To Marc,

Blessings!

Death Knocking, Life Calling

THE AMAZING TRUE STORY
OF RANDY AND MARY ANN GALLAWAY

Randy Gallaway

John 15:7

By Randy and Mary Ann Gallaway
with Bear Mills

Forward by Chris Galanos,
Pastor of Experience Life Church

For information, inquiries, and speaking events, contact:
Randy Gallaway at randyga@pobox.com or
Bear Mills at wwbearmills@gmail.com.

ISBN: 1502469243
ISBN 13: 9781502469243
Library of Congress Control Number: 2014917596
CreateSpace Independent Publishing Platform
North Charleston, South Carolina

I am alive today because so many people prayed for me and gave me their love, prayers, and encouragement. This book is dedicated to all the people who helped me survive and recover. Most crucial of all are two very special women, my mom, Virginia Moore Gallaway, and my amazing wife Mary Ann Milliken Gallaway. My mom was my encourager from birth, through and past the accident, until she died at age seventy-three. Since I met Mary Ann, she has been the love of my life. She stood beside me in every adventure and crisis for forty years, never wavering in her love and support. I am truly blessed.

Randy Gallaway
November, 2014

Table of Contents

Introduction

My daughter, Sarah, was a student at Texas Tech University in Lubbock when she took a job as an administrative assistant to Randy and Mary Ann Gallaway. One day she called me and said, "You need to meet Randy. His story is like a movie. In fact, you need to help him turn it into a book. Then the right people can read it and turn it into a movie. It's incredible."

My novel, *The Ecuadorian Deception*, was at a crucial juncture and I didn't need another project. Nonetheless, based on Sarah's recommendation, I made time to drive to Lubbock and meet Randy. His story was, if anything, even more amazing than Sarah had conveyed.

From a journalistic or literary point of view, it contains all the ingredients of a great saga: a noble hero, a tragedy of almost unspeakable magnitude, a good woman (two, in fact: Randy's mom and later his wife, Mary Ann) who perseveres and inspires, and sub-plots circling the main story like planets orbiting the sun, each lending their own gravitational force.

Over the next three years, Randy, Mary Ann, and I spent count-less hours together. Then I would write and my wife Caryl would read what we'd done. Next, she and I would sit down and discuss how best to move forward. Her contributions are a valuable part of the behind-the-scenes work on this book. I am honored to be the midwife who helped Randy and Mary Ann give birth to this project. And thanks to our daughter, Sarah, for making the introduction. You are a pearl.

Bear Mills

Forward

I remember the first time I heard Randy's story. I was shocked and saddened to learn about all he went through. But what was stunning was the way in which he talked about it. As I listened, I thought about how I would respond in similar circumstances. It's hard to imagine how anyone could find joy in such a devastating tragedy. Randy could've let his accident ruin the rest of his life, but he didn't. He wasn't bitter. He wasn't angry. I feel like he responded kind of like Jesus would have in a similar situation. Through this great tragedy, God has given him a great story, and this story has changed many people's lives, including mine.

Randy's response to his tragedy reminds me of something James encouraged his scattered church to do when he said, "Dear brothers and sisters, when troubles come your way, consider it an opportunity for great joy. For you know that when your faith is tested, your endurance has a chance to grow. So let it grow, for when your endurance is fully developed, you will be perfect and complete, needing nothing." (James 1:2-4) We all need examples of what it looks like to consider trouble an opportunity for great joy. Randy's story is just such an instance.

Randy is a hero to our whole family. All of us referred to him as "our pastor" because he really did lead us, like a shepherd leads

His sheep. My dad used to always say, "Randy is my pastor," even though Randy wasn't even the pastor of the church. Still, he was a pastor in the truest sense of the word. He is someone who cares for and leads other people into God's best for their lives. He was and is easy for all of us to follow. Anyone who has known Randy over the years wanted to be like him. That's what a pastor is supposed to be like, isn't it?

Randy is the kind of guy you just want to follow around and watch. Whether he's leading a Bible study or telling someone about Jesus, he's captivating. When he talks, people listen. He presents the truth filled with grace. Anytime I needed advice or someone to talk to, Randy was always eager to listen and share. A few years ago, I had the privilege of being on the same church staff as Randy. His office door was always open and anyone was free to walk in.

Then, in 2007, I called Randy before I started Experience Life Church. I wanted his advice. The town we both lived in really didn't have many "church plants." I was unsure about how a new church would be received. As a pastor, Randy helped me think through the risks and the potential rewards and encouraged me to pursue what God had placed on my heart. I'll never forget that.

Randy believed in me, and there wasn't really much to believe in at that point. I ended up starting the church and we've now seen over eight thousand people commit their life to Christ and over four thousand have been baptized. That's all happened in just under seven years. I'm not sure if Experience Life would be here without people like Randy and others that encouraged me to follow God's leading regardless of the cost.

As you read Randy's story, be prepared to cry, laugh, and leave completely changed. If you're looking for a pastor to follow, follow Randy. When troubles come your way, and they do for all of us, follow Randy's example. I thank God for Randy's influence in my life and I hope that millions of people all across the world get to read this story and be impacted by it in the way I was.

Chris Galanos
Lead Pastor
ExperienceLifeNow.com

Chapter 1

THE DAY THAT CHANGED
EVERYTHING

Randy

It was 5 a.m. Sunday morning, March 27, 1966. During that era, the world was focused on The Beatles, a TV show called *Man From U.N.C.L.E.*, and the Vietnam War. Not me. I was focused on getting up and going into work for a couple of hours. Though I was only in high school, I was working part-time for the same company where my dad was an engineer.

I was eighteen and would graduate in two months. My dad helped me get the job. It was a factory that started manufacturing weapons during World War II and now made five-inch artillery shells for the Navy, along with oilfield equipment. My job was to assist a man named George and learn all I could from him.

I planned to take care of the assignment they had for us, and then leave in plenty of time to make it to church for worship and Sunday school. I've always had a big appetite. My mom knew that and made up some pancake batter the night before. As I put the batter on the griddle, I thought about my day.

My usual job was to carry conduit, test electrical circuits, hook up machines that had been disconnected over the years, and repair equipment. But that Sunday I was getting to work on the towers. That was very exciting for a young kid.

The smell of pancakes filled the kitchen. It was a cold March morning, so I was dressed in layers, wearing a t-shirt, work shirt, sweatshirt, and jacket. A good breakfast would also help me stay warm. After I cleaned up my dishes, I got in my car and headed out.

The electrical foreman had asked George to come in and do some work on the towers where all the high voltage electricity came into the building from the power lines overhead. The company, American Manufacturing, was housed in a large, corrugated steel building with a sloped roof that was two to three stories tall. As we went up there, I saw steel pipes coming out through the roof and going up maybe twenty feet. They had attachments where the high voltage electrical wires came into the poles. There were switches that could be cut off right there, but sometimes they worked and sometimes they didn't.

You had to have a ten-foot insulated pole to pull those switches. Above that were wires going up to the crossbeams and three large wires that came in from Texas Electric. It was kind of a hodge-podge of wires going every direction. The problem was the wiring was overloaded, so we were going to replace all the transformers. The primary work was done the previous weekend. Now they needed us to work on the connections. It was a special honor for a young guy like me to work on such a project.

As I said, this was during the Vietnam War, so the draft was taking a lot of people out of the workforce. The factory had swollen to about three thousand employees and they were hiring everybody they could find. The military needed weapons, so they were cranking up a part of the factory that had been mothballed since the Korean War. As part of activating the area, I was hired to help George on the electrical team.

2

Of course, I respected electricity. Even one hundred and ten volts in a house can kill you. The man who did my initial training was Mr. Byrd, an older electrician. He'd done it for years and was very careful. He taught me to be careful. When equipment was malfunctioning, we would first check to see if the machine was getting power. When you find what's not getting power, you've found what needs to be fixed. On new construction, we would run new wires and conduits and then check both the wiring and the circuits. On older equipment, a lot of times you didn't know where the wires went; you didn't know what was connected to what. There were huge bundles of wires that would split off in every direction and go off to relays. It was like a mass of spaghetti.

That's the kind of thing we worked on each day. The idea was for us to figure out which wires weren't working. We were supposed to check for what was wrong. Then someone would turn off the power so we could do our repairs. When the power was turned back on, we would see if the problem was fixed.

This job fit perfectly with my plans to graduate from high school and then go to college to major in mechanical engineering. By being in the electrical department, I had the chance to study every machine in the whole factory. For me, working on the electrical system was the launch pad to understanding the mechanics of every machine. On this project I was being asked to come in on a Sunday and go up to the top of the factory building. I was helping George Haas, a married man with five children. He was a rough-and-tumble, blue-collar fellow. Once he told me, "I have a deal with God. He leaves me alone and I leave Him alone." I liked him a lot and tried to learn all I could from him, even though we really saw the world differently.

George had been a lineman, but he took a job at the plant so he didn't have to travel all the time and be away from his wife and children. Even though the factory didn't pay very much, all the overtime added up. If you were tough enough to work the long hours and stand the summer heat and winter cold, it was a good job. George was chosen for this assignment because he had experience on high lines at his previous company.

Each work day began with us going to the electrical department's shop and putting on our uniforms. Then, because it was cold, we put on overalls for warmth. After that, we put on belts that held all our tools. A lot of times we were up in the rafters or on rolling cranes. We had to have our tools right there, self-contained in leather pouches on our belts.

As electricians, we didn't need heavy wrenches and a big tool box. Most jobs involved wires, so we could complete the task with slip-joint pliers or a screwdriver and electrical tape. We also had electrical meters to check the voltage. Everything we carried had slip-on insulated handles. The insulation was good up to four-hundred and eighty volts, which was the limit inside the factory. But up on the towers, the lines that were leading to the transformers had thirteen-thousand-five-hundred volts.

The foreman of the plant, someone we'll call "Sam," was a grizzled old man and not very pleasant. Sam helped start the factory thirty-two years earlier and had been the number-two man ever since. He was the general foreman over the machine shop and manager over the electrical shop. However, the truth was that he wasn't an electrician and didn't know too much about it. Sam didn't follow safety protocols or let anyone else follow them because safety protocols slowed things down. There were none of the safety precautions that should have been in place.

If anybody asked Sam about safety, he would say, "I turn on the power and I turn it off. That's all." That morning he had the power turned off. George and I were sent up to the top of the building.

4

We were both up on the tower at what were called the high side switches. The switches sit above a huge transformer bank at the top of the foundry building. Keep in mind that when Sam told us the power coming into the plant was off, we had to take him at his word.

We also weren't in a position to turn off the high line power ourselves. The foreman, Sam, assured us the power was turned off upstream at the property line of the factory. We checked the four eighty volts and they were off. While we were working, Sam either forgot we were up there or he was just careless. He ordered the contractor who had turned the power off to turn it back on.

When that happened, it instantly burned George to a crisp. I believe he was killed that second. Getting hit with that much power is like being struck by lightning. The difference is that a lightning bolt is just a flash and then it's over. In our case, the power lines just kept delivering power until it literally melted the fuses. The jolt knocked George three stories to the ground below. There was some question about whether the electricity or the fall killed him. The thing is that he was dead by the time somebody got to him.

The same electricity pulsed through my whole body. It felt like it was happening in slow motion. Fortunately, I was wearing brand new boots with rubber soles, so the electricity didn't go through my feet. If I had ever punctured the soles, it might have gone through my legs because I was standing on that metal derrick. But those boots saved my feet. However, one of my knees was close to the metal. Electricity jumped from my knee to the derrick, setting my pants leg on fire. That burn was minor, compared to what was happening in my upper body.

Electricity shot through my chest, immediately destroying my right arm completely. From my elbow, the electricity jumped to my steel pliers and melted them. It then shot to my ribcage, burning a six-inch hole in my right side and scorching two ribs.

Next, it passed through my body under my left arm. It arced there and burned a hole about the size of an orange. The same thing happened at every joint in my upper body. It destroyed the tendon and blood supply on my lower left arm. My wristwatch exploded and my left hand was burned beyond saving. How in the world did so much power – enough power to melt steel pliers – pass through my chest without destroying my heart, lungs, and internal organs?

As I said, George was thrown three stories to the ground below. The surge of power also ejected me from the tower. I tumbled through the air and landed on a corrugated tin roof about twenty feet below. I was conscious until I slammed into the roof, hitting my head. At that point, I blacked out. I was aware of everything happening to me up to that point. I remember the electricity, the explosion through my body, the fire. I also remember falling. Then I was knocked out for a time, but I'm not sure whether it was for seconds or minutes.

There was a skeleton crew of men on the ground that Sunday morning, as well as other men working outside moving steel and that kind of thing. Those men on the ground heard a big popping sound and looked up to see the explosion. They saw George and me falling through the air. George fell all the way to the ground. If I had, I would also have been killed. But the men who looked up knew approximately where I landed from the trajectory of how I was sailing through the air.

They found a service ladder fixed at the end of the building. It probably took them two or three minutes to get to me. When they did, they tried to put the fire out. It was a cold day and they were doing heavy work, so each employee had gloves on. They used those to smother the fire. But what they didn't know was that while my outerwear was no longer on fire, the layers underneath were still smoldering. In other words, I was still on fire.

I was crying out for help the second I regained consciousness. The first thing I remember was seeing their horrified faces. They were crying and pounding on my clothes, trying to put out the fire. The first face I saw was Mr. Byrd, the electrician who trained me. He was sobbing.

They had no equipment like a fire extinguisher or even dirt to put out the fire. They did the best they could with their bare hands and gloves. They were afraid to move me, so I was lying on the tin roof with my clothes still burning. Most of my back was covered in second and third degree burns.

By the time the fire department came, I was in and out of consciousness. Years later I learned it was a rookie firefighting crew. This was their first rescue. They laid me in a stretcher made of something like chicken wire and strapped me in. It took them a while to get me down because they didn't know which power lines running between the different buildings were live and which ones weren't.

They didn't want to take a chance of bumping the basket into a live wire. When I came to for a moment, the pain was simply beyond description. And the fire underneath me was still burning the skin on my back as it smoldered in my clothes. I remember the terror of being lowered over the edge of the building on that stretcher, dangling by a rope. It wasn't a smooth descent. It felt like they were dropping me. I would fall a couple of feet and then stop and then it would happen again, all the way to the ground.

They finally got me down and loaded into the ambulance. At that time, an ambulance was just a station wagon with an oxygen bottle. The firefighters threw me in there and raced a hundred miles an hour to John Peter Smith Hospital. It was the largest hospital in the area.

My dad had actually been at the factory working in the engineering department that morning. It was on the complete other side of the complex. Lights all over the factory, even in his office, flickered when the explosion happened. He knew I was working on the electrical wires and that something had occurred. When he got word I had been electrocuted, he got in his car and tried to follow the ambulance to the hospital. They were going so fast, he couldn't keep up.

By the time I was taken into the emergency room, news reporters monitoring police band radios heard about what happened. Apparently, there was radio traffic about a factory explosion. I still remember coming into the hospital in that condition. A reporter was trying to interview me while they rolled me into the emergency room. I just kept saying, "Go away, go away." Every time I said it, he would ask me another question. He was totally heartless. Everyone thought I was dying and he wanted to get an interview. Totally heartless.

The doctors on duty found my driver's license and began to call people to let them know what happened. My dad came in a little bit later and he also began to call family members. Relatives from all over were called in. My mom received two calls, one from somebody at the factory, then one from my dad. She was too distraught to drive, but a friend from church drove her to the hospital.

When Mom arrived at the hospital to be with my dad, the news wasn't good. After a few hours a doctor came out and said, "This kid cannot live. There's simply no way he can make it. Fifty-five percent of his body has third degree burns. Some of his bones are even burned. "

He continued, saying, "His ribs are charred; his internal organs are probably cooked. His urine looks like chocolate. He is so full of dead tissue that his kidneys are bound to fail. There is simply no way to keep him alive. He has twenty-four hours max before everything shuts down. You need to say your goodbyes."

Chapter 2

GOD HASN'T SPOKEN YET

Randy

I attended church at Oak Knoll Baptist. Services were already in session when word of the explosion reached them. They simply stopped what they were doing and everyone started praying for me. After prayer, everyone made their way to the hospital. And you know what? The pastor, Jarvis Philpot, simply refused to believe I was going to die. He spread the word, though, that I was in dire need of divine intervention.

As the news got around – and remember, this was long before the time of cell phones, Facebook, and text messages – people poured into the hospital to pray. In the emergency room, I was in the last stages of shock before death. However, Dr. Valentine Gracia, drove over from another hospital after hearing about my accident on the radio. When he arrived, he found me unable to breathe. He immediately performed an emergency tracheotomy by cutting a hole into my windpipe and inserting a tube. The opening let air pass so I could breathe again. Without that, I would have died right then.

Later that day I was moved over to All Saints Hospital, because that was where Dr. Gracia practiced. All these people from church had gathered at John Peter Smith to pray for me and be with my mom and dad. When they heard I'd been moved, they simply relocated their prayer meeting to All Saints. The waiting room was overwhelmed. There were so many people that the group had to go out into the parking lot.

Of course, I didn't know it at the time, but while I was inside fighting to stay alive and the doctors were trying to figure out what to do, the people from church were holding a prayer meeting in the parking lot. Days later, a friend put a guestbook in the waiting room. It showed that one hundred and sixty-one people came to pray for me at the hospital. That didn't count all the people who came to pray before the book was set out, or the ones who were praying for me in other places. Every time someone said something about me dying, Pastor Philpot would say, "God hasn't spoken yet."

That took a lot of faith on the part of Pastor Philpot, because the news that day was really grim. It took seventeen units of blood to keep me alive the next twenty-four hours. I was bleeding profusely from all the burns. They had to continually give me transfusions to keep me going.

Here's something really amazing that happened during that horrible period. The employees who worked at the factory were mostly rough guys. They liked to brag about how much liquor they could put away, how drunk they got the night before, or how they didn't take flak from anyone.

Being a Christian, and vocal about my faith, I had tried to tell them about Jesus and my relationship with Him. As far as I could tell, not a one of them listened. But here's the thing; when word got around about what happened to me, those men were among the first to line up and donate blood to keep me alive.

For three days, the people from Oak Knoll, along with family members, filled the waiting room and parking lot. They were praying and asking God to spare my life. God did intervene and kept me alive.

Everyone had heard that the doctors said I wouldn't last more than twenty-four hours. But forty-eight hours passed and I was still alive. Then another twenty-four hours passed and I hadn't died yet. It was at this point that the doctors had to make some difficult decisions. They told my parents that if I was to have any chance at survival, it was necessary to amputate my entire right arm to the shoulder and most of my left arm. By that time, gangrene had set in because there was no blood getting to my left hand or entire right arm. The veins were burned in two. Fortunately, the bicep muscle of my left arm was still getting blood. The crisis became, "Do we wait for gangrene to kill him or do we let him die from organ failure?"

The only way to give me a few more hours was to amputate my right arm and left hand. They were nothing more than cooked bone and flesh hanging from my shoulders. I had a double death sentence. Which would kill me first, the gangrene or the burns?

However, even if they amputated my arms, the doctors said I was far from out of the woods. They were still saying there was no way my organs could last. However, Dr. Gracia wasn't ready to give up. He was an expert at burns; a plastic surgeon who had emigrated from Mexico. He called in four or five other specialists. I had hung in there the first day, second day, and third day. They kept waiting for me to die. To this day I am convinced it was the prayers of all those people in the parking lots and waiting rooms that kept me alive long enough for the doctor's to talk about amputating. The thinking was that if they could get rid of the gangrene and a big percentage of the burns, I would have at least a ghost of a chance.

Dr. Gracia conferred with the other doctors, including some who specialized in internal organs, one who specialized in chest surgery, and an orthopedist. There were all these different doctors because they feared my organs might fail during surgery. There was also the issue of my burned ribs and the possible need to re-inflate my lungs if they collapsed from the hole in my side. Dr. Gracia told them that if I was going to live, it was imperative they operate right then.

But the other doctors didn't agree. They believed it was all a waste of time and I was going to die anyway. All of them said no, they shouldn't operate, as did the anesthesiologist. That anesthesiologist was unwavering in saying he wouldn't cooperate. Dr. Gracia kept saying, "He's lived this long. Let's at least give him a chance."

Over their objections, Dr. Gracia had me prepped and taken into surgery. But the other doctors still weren't signing off on it. The other doctors' opposition to surgery hadn't changed. At one point things got heated. Dr. Gracia was literally ready to fight for the surgery. The anesthesiologist was just as insistent that he wouldn't cooperate and put me under. He didn't want me to die after he had put me on anesthesia for fear he would be blamed.

The other doctors were wavering back and forth. Dr. Gracia became so angry, so adamant that they had to give me every chance to live, that he grabbed the anesthesiologist and said, "Put him to sleep." The anesthesiologist said, "No." The argument grew more intense. Dr. Gracia actually knocked the other doctor to the floor and began to wrestle with him. Then Dr. Gracia hit him right in the face with his fist! Talk about somebody willing to fight for your life. The anesthesiologist changed his mind.

Let me jump ahead just a second to tell you something very interesting. A quarter of a century later, when I was working in Canada, I met a guy named Sam Fort. At the time I was electro-cuted, Sam was attending seminary in Fort Worth. He also had a job working at All Saints Hospital drawing blood.

Sam was one of the people who took care of me. Talk about a small world. When we met in Canada, Sam told me he had absolutely hated coming to draw my blood because I was already in horrible pain and the blood draw made it worse. But it was his job, so he came every single hour.

During our Canada encounter, Sam told me when he would enter my room he would start praying for me. So his prayers were added to all the others that were going up on my behalf. As Sam and I recounted those days, each from our own perspective, he asked me, "Do you know why the anesthesiologist refused to put you to sleep?

Then he explained, "Eight weeks earlier the anesthesiologist had put a healthy eighteen-year-old kid to sleep for some minor surgery. The kid died." Sam explained that because I was still in shock, and in such bad shape, the anesthesiologist was convinced the medicine he would have to give me to put me under would actually kill me.

Shortly before my accident, the anesthesiologist had learned that he was being sued for negligence over the death of that eighteen year old. Since he believed I was going to die anyway, regardless of what he did, he didn't want to put himself in further liability with another death on his record.

While I understand where that anesthesiologist was coming from, I am so grateful to Dr. Gracia for refusing to give up on me. Men who stand up for what they believe in are rare. He had faith when other people said it was useless to exert any special effort. After all, I was just going to die anyway.

When the anesthesiologist relented, the other doctors agreed to pitch in and help. One of them was Dr. Jack West, who had battlefield experience from being a surgeon in Vietnam. He knew all about artificial limbs. As they discussed cutting off my arms, he told the others they should work to save my left elbow. Even though the bicep and tendon were destroyed and much of the supporting tissue and blood supply were gone, he advocated saving the joint at all costs. He said that was vital if I was ever going to be able to drive or use an artificial limb. The artificial limb had to have something to which it could attach.

Dr. West knew I needed that elbow joint to have any chance of living independently. The left elbow and four inches of forearm was the difference between having a chance at living on my own one day or always being in custodial care. I know there are some people born without arms who learn to use their feet to do a lot of things, but by the time I was eighteen, my hips wouldn't have cooperated, so that wasn't a possibility for me.

They put me to sleep and did the amputations. Once all the gangrene and burnt cells were gone, they cauterized the bleeding in the upper part of what was left. That was all good news, but you couldn't have convinced me of it at the time.

When I came to, the pain was excruciating. I don't remember screaming, but I wanted to scream. With the tracheotomy, I couldn't speak, scream, or anything. My body had some chance, because I came out of the surgery alive. For the next three weeks I was in and out of consciousness. When I was awake, the pain was so intense, so horrible; it was straight out of a never-ending nightmare. The only thing was that I couldn't wake up and make it end.

I couldn't speak because of the tracheotomy. When I would move my mouth, the nurses would cover the hole and I could whisper. They used the hole to suction my lungs multiple times a day. They were taking fluid off my lungs. It felt like I was being kicked in the chest the whole time it was going on.

Of course, the factory where my dad and I worked, where the accident happened, was very nervous about the financial and legal consequences of the accident. I didn't know it at the time, but between the amputations, some insurance men representing the factory actually came to the hospital and tried to get my family to settle. How much were they willing to pay? A flat amount of twelve thousand dollars. Even in the 1960s, with all the medical bills we were facing, that was not very much money.

That made things very tough for my parents. My mom and dad both knew that if they chose to sue the factory for negligence, medical bills, the whole thing, my dad would lose his job. And there weren't protections back then against retaliation like there are now. My mom wanted to sue, but my dad wanted to protect his job. It created a rift in their marriage that was never repaired. But my father was resolute about not suing.

They also felt stress and anguish over me having both arms removed and the fact I might die anyway. They didn't know how they were going to pay the medical bills. If I lived, it would be without my arms. If they sued, my dad would also most likely be without a job.

Something else to keep in mind is that this was happening in the 1960s. Every day the news carried stories of young people experimenting with drugs, overdosing, and dying. Everyone wanted to make sure the young people around them weren't getting hooked on drugs. So what did that have to do with me?

The hospital was afraid to give me too much pain medication because they didn't want me to be addicted. Since none of them had ever been burned like I was, they had no idea the suffering I was going through. The pain was grueling. In fact, it was so bad, I started to hallucinate. I saw bugs and spiders crawling all around my room. There was terror. I couldn't get away. Of course, they were only hallucinations, but they went on for hours and seemed very real. And even when the hospital staff did give me pain medi-cation, it was not anywhere close to providing any real relief.

One of the medicines they tried was simple aspirin. It wasn't strong enough to relieve the pain and it created another problem. I've always had negative reactions to aspirin. It actually seemed to amplify the agony; to make it worse. I also started having terrible fits of uncontrollable nervousness. I was a Christian, and I believe I was a very strong Christian. However, with the hallucinations, the pain, everything that was happening, I began to say, "God, just let me die."

I started saying things to God like, "I know I'm a Christian. Christ died for my sins. I'm saved. I truly believe in you and have tried to live for you. Please let me come to heaven. Please stop this suffering."

Since I'm here, you know God didn't grant my request to die. But there was no rest, day or night. I couldn't sleep. It really was constant, agonizing pain. I've read that burn victims in war will beg their fellow soldiers to kill them. I understand why. It was beyond horrible.

While God didn't let me die, He did send someone to teach me how powerful it can be when we pray for one another. One of the nurses in the Intensive Care Unit, a woman named Becky Short, was a Christian. She heard me praying for God to let me die. She came to my bedside with a different prayer. She prayed for God to give me the grace to bear the pain or take the pain away.

God honored her prayer. In that instant, I passed out. When I awoke, the pain was never again to the point of wanting to die. Some way, somehow, God gave me the grace to endure. Nurse Short was married to a man attending Southwestern Seminary. Through her and her husband, the whole seminary heard about what had happened to me. They joined their prayers with those of the people at Oak Knoll Baptist. It was at that point I truly slept for the first time in three weeks. Things were still miserable, but God allowed me to sleep and not just lay there in torment. Even in the midst of that horror, God met my need.

Chapter 3

FOUNDATIONS

Randy

When you go through something like being electrocuted, it makes you think about what happens after you die. But it also makes you think about your life. How had I come to a point where I could be so sure, in spite of the circumstances, that there was a God who had a plan for me? How had there come to be so many committed Christians surrounding me with prayer twenty-four hours a day for weeks and months? What about my parents? What was all this doing to them?

My mom and dad, Ginger and Norris, originally met at the University of Texas in the 1940s. My dad was studying engineering. When World War II came along, dad joined the Army Air Corps. He became a fighter pilot in the Pacific, piloting P-61 Night Fighters.

Dad had always been really skinny. So skinny, in fact, he had to eat extra meals for several weeks to gain enough weight to get into the Army Air Corps. He was really proud to fly a P-61. They were the fastest prop planes in World War II, loaded with guns and cannons and painted jet black. They had two two-thousand horse power radial engines and could fly higher than other planes. In fact, they could get up to forty-thousand feet or more. Each P-61 carried a crew of three: a pilot, co-pilot, and tail gunner.

The planes were designed for long-range flight over the Pacific, the Yellow Sea, and the Sea of Japan. They had extra fuel tanks to help them go farther. But during combat, those fuel tanks could be discarded to make the planes go faster. It also helped to make them less flammable when taking enemy fire.

They could go up so high they were actually above other planes. During this time, locating enemy aircraft was mostly done visually by the plane's crew. Therefore, the P-61 had a real advantage. They could get up above everything else to look for Japanese planes, ships, or convoys. The P-61 was also the first fighter with forward-looking radar. A large radar dome was located in the front of the plane in an elongated nose. This necessitated twin engines located in twin booms with a long, narrow cabin and fuselage behind the radar.

My dad really loved those planes. I remember him telling me all about them. One of the saddest, most frustrating memories for him was seeing the Army Air Corps just dumping those beautiful planes off of the end of aircraft carriers into the sea after the war. It was a waste of beautiful machinery, not to mention taxpayer dollars. Seeing things like that made my father very skeptical of the government, especially the military, from then on. But that wasn't the only scar the war left on Dad.

It wasn't long after he got home that the problems started. Today they would call it Post-Traumatic Stress Disorder or PTSD. Of course, back in that day, people didn't call it anything. Most people simply believed men went off to war and then came home and resumed their lives. All the horrible things that soldiers saw and the people they killed, that wasn't supposed to affect them. But it did.

On the surface, everything might have seemed fine. He and my mom had gotten married during the war. They lived in Austin, where they attended college. Dad managed to hide the psychological issues he was having and became a field engineer, first for Magnolia Oil Company and then for Mobil Oil Company. During the week, he would work really long hours and travel a great deal. My dad also liked to work on cars.

We were, in a lot of ways, a typical family. I was the first of three children, born a couple of years after the war in September, 1947. My parents liked to take me to the park near whatever little house they were renting at the time. However, there would be some serious problems later.

My mother became a Christian when she was eighteen. She was a tremendously loving person. I vividly remember her ability to inspire, encourage, and affirm her children. She gave her total attention to being a good mom. When my brother and sister were born, she did the same thing for all three of us.

Mom was the one who helped us kids develop our theological underpinnings. She helped build our personalities and self-confidence. I was really shy, so that was extremely important. She taught us to put our trust in God and helped us learn to love people and treat life as precious.

During those early years, my grandmother came to live with us. She was a very loving person, as well. My grandmother would entertain us by singing and rocking us in her rocking chair. That part of my childhood was warm and affirming.

About that time, we moved from Austin to San Antonio. Our house had bricks that formed a flower bed around the front. Each brick had three holes in them and the holes were filled with cement. One day I took a little toy hammer and started to peck away at the little cement patches. I was very proud of myself because I succeeded in knocking the cement out of each one of those little holes.

Boy was I in trouble when my parents found out. My father became so angry he lost control. That was my first experience with his PTSD-fueled fury. It was a look into what was going on in his head and it wasn't good.

While my mother had dedicated her life to Christ, my father, chose to turn away from the Lord. He just wanted to be a successful mechanical engineer and thought that was enough. During the early years of my life, I had a pretty good relationship with my dad. Even though he traveled a lot with his job, he did try to spend some time with me when he was home. He seemed to take great joy in being with me and in teaching me things.

Being an engineer, he was fascinated by how things worked. Whenever something broke around the house, he would take it apart. Even though I was really little he would demonstrate piece by piece how it all went together. A lot of our time together was Dad showing me how things worked, how they should work, and how to fix whatever was wrong. Being an engineer, he loved physics and mechanical things. He loved to explain theories to me in detail. Probably by the time I was in first grade, I knew more about engineering than a lot of adults.

Another way my father and I bonded was over cars. I quickly learned to recognize and name every car on the road. Studebakers, Dodges, Fords, Pontiacs, Chevrolets, I could name them all. I could also tell you the model and often what year it was by looking at the body style.

But no matter how good our relationship was in that way, no matter how good things were with work or his family, my dad was always struggling mentally and emotionally with memories from the war. He liked to drink and would spend a lot of time in bars.

My mom never liked that scene. She particularly hated it when her brilliant husband was inebriated and talked like inebriated people do.

See, with dad there was no such thing as just having a drink or two. He was all in when it came to alcohol. Since Mom wouldn't go out with him, he went drinking alone. Even as a child, I remember being so confused about why my smart dad would come home acting so sluggish and muddled and, sometimes, angry.

Over the years we learned that early evenings were happy times. Those were the times when Dad was still sober. But as the night wore on and my dad drank more, some small thing would make him angry. To escape arguments and half-sober lectures about who knows what, my little brother and sister and I would play outside or stay with our friends as long as possible.

One time Dad was out drinking at this bar and they had a Thanksgiving turkey giveaway. Well, my dad won. The only catch was that the turkey was still alive! I'm sure that was tremendously funny to the people at the bar. "Hey, you won a Thanksgiving turkey for your family. What are you going to name it?" So dad brought home a live turkey and it became our pet, living out in the back yard. But as it got closer and closer to Thanksgiving, I realized my pet turkey was going to be Thanksgiving dinner.

It was more than a five-year-old could handle. From an early age I've had a very soft heart, not wanting to see animals or people suffer in any way. I cried and begged Dad not to kill the turkey. So he let the turkey live and bought another one from the store that was already killed and cleaned for our dinner.

So my dad was drinking all the time. It was his way of dealing with all the frustrations in his life and the memories of war. Sometimes he took his frustrations out on me, like he did when I hammered out the mortar in the bricks in front of our house. I remember one time when he was under a lot of pressure at work. I had gotten into some of his work materials and had written on some sales pads. I really got a spanking when he got home. It was the only time he ever spanked me, but it was a doozey. It was the spanking of a lifetime. I couldn't understand why he was so upset with me. It was just stress from work that boiled over.

Of course, I was only a very small child at the time. I knew there were problems with my dad's behavior and that it often involved alcohol, but didn't really understand what was going on. A few months after that, my father had a nervous breakdown. It was a very dark time for our family.

We lived in a small frame house on the outskirts of Temple, Texas. Dad was having delusions and becoming extremely para-noid. Even as a child I could tell something was seriously wrong. The situation deteriorated very rapidly.

One day he announced that it was going to be my job to build a swimming pool in our back yard. I was very young, maybe six, and he handed me a shovel. He said I was to go out into the back yard and dig a swimming pool. He wasn't kidding. He turned on the water and got the yard all muddy and told me to start digging. I was confused and scared, but I tried to please him. But did he really want his little boy digging a real swimming pool? He was having this grandiose delusion that he could do anything and that I could do anything, too. He wanted to prove it by having me dig an entire swimming pool.

My mom would just cry and cry. I think it's one of the most dif-ficult things in the world to deal with an irrational person. That's what she was trying to do. It's what we, as children, were trying to do. But you can't have rational discussions with an irrational person. Mom kept begging him to let go of this idea. She had to get good at refocusing him on something else. Maybe it was when we got the water bill or the fact our entire back yard was a sticky, muddy quagmire for days and days, but he finally moved on to some other idea and I was released from this impossible task.

At times he would be very focused on one particular thing, like an invention he was working on. He would rant about it for hours and hours and hours. His whole countenance would change from loving dad to authoritarian power figure. He lectured us without end, going on and on about the same thing. He would make us sit down and listen to hours of lectures about this or that. I can still remember he would be going on and on and then say, "Always have a plan B. Always have a plan B."

Mom couldn't reason with him when he got like that. We learned to just cower and listen. If you interrupted him or tried to agree with him by saying, "I understand," he would start all over from the very beginning. So we just sat there for hours and listened and didn't speak a word. Finally, he would get tired of talking. He would leave the house for beer. That would give us a little bit of a break. But we also feared what would happen when he returned. It actually became a relief when he would stay out all night.

It was very hard to tell what might set him off on one of his tirades. Because my dad traveled a great deal, mom saved and saved and bought a beautiful suitcase. The suitcase made him furious. Evidently he interpreted it as Mom telling him we didn't want him at home anymore. When he would fly into a tirade, the safest thing to do was to not do anything

Of course, I was a little child and wondered why my dad was acting that way. When things were really bad, Mom would just explain that he was really confused from being in the war. She would tell my little brother and sister and me to be patient and pray for things to get better. That gave us a little hope. Often, though, we just had to tough it out through the bad times. As a child, I was aware of how un-right things were, but I was powerless to do anything about it. In his diminished state, Dad also began having an affair with a woman who lived nearby. This pushed my mom to the edge of her patience with Dad.

Occasionally Dad would be in a good mood and try to do something nice for Mom. After the birth of my little brother, Dad was excited about getting the house ready for Mom and baby Rex to come home. He really threw himself into cleaning the house and waxing all the floors. The house was beautiful and Mom was pleased. The floors shined like mirrors, but were also slick as glass. Mom was carrying baby Rex and slipped and fell.

I can still remember being scared for her safety and for my newborn brother, who she was holding when she fell. I was crying. My mom was hurt. And then there was Dad. It was just another frustration piled on top of all the others. He had worked so hard to do something nice for her and it all seemed to turn to ashes.

We went through some very difficult times as a family. As things got worse, my mom had to call Uncle Ben, dad's brother, for help. Uncle Ben had a family and lived in Weatherford, Texas. He would drive down to our house, which was a long way. Ben was the kind of man I'm sure my dad wished he could have been. Uncle Ben was a real hero of mine. When things got really tough, Ben would show up to help out.

Looking at Uncle Ben and my dad through the prism of the years is kind of an interesting study of life with Christ and life without Christ. Ben was my dad's younger brother. He only got to finish high school, whereas my dad got to finish college. In World War II they were both stationed on the same island in the Pacific. Dad got married during the war to my mom. Ben got married right after the war.

So their lives were very similar and they experienced a lot of the same things. One difference, though, was that Ben became a Christian. My dad had a college education, but he rejected Christ. Uncle Ben became a deacon and a wonderful family man.

Basically, Uncle Ben knew God and God knew him. In spite of his lack of formal education, Ben became an advisor and friend to pastors. He was also one of the most respected men in Weatherford at that time. He might not have had a college degree, but he had God-given wisdom.

During one of my dad's delusional periods, he told Mom and Ben that he had to get a very important message to the president. Ben told Dad he would take him somewhere so he could tell the right people. Ben convinced Dad that these "right people" would be able to pass the message along.

He told my dad to get in the back of the car and stay down. It was terrifying for a first grader to see his father go out of control and begin to do bizarre things. It was always a relief when Uncle Ben showed up. This time, Uncle Ben knew that the "right people" were at a veteran's hospital that focused on mental health.

Because my dad was a veteran he was placed in the Veterans Hospital in Galveston, Texas. Uncle Ben drove all night to take Dad there. My father spent the entire time ducked down in the back of the car, hiding from people whom he believed were out to get him.

Dad was in the hospital for six months. The people there said my dad's mental and emotional health were in such bad shape, he would never be able to work again. This was quite a shock to Mom, who had dedicated her whole life to being a housewife and mother. We had no money coming in and no prospects for any. In spite of everything, though, she remained strong, at least in front of us.

I remember her loading us up and taking us to see Dad in the hospital. She was so loyal and worked hard to stay connected and help him get well. One time we were getting ready to go and Mom was all dressed up. The back door to our house stuck, but there wasn't anybody around to fix it. Mom was trying to close it and lock it. She pushed on it hard with her shoulder. The glass broke and a shard plunged into her shoulder near the collarbone. She pulled out the glass, put a bandage on it and went on to drive us all the way from central Texas to Galveston down on the coast, though she had that serious cut.

My mother was brave and strong and optimistic. I think I got a lot of my optimism in life from her, learning to trust God during difficult times. That was something Mother always modeled.

Mom came from a large extended family. When they saw that she had no way to take care of her children, they chipped in to help with the finances. Before any of these issues with my dad became common knowledge, her family had a plan. Each child who graduated from college would go out and start making money. Then they would help the next younger one go to college if they wanted to go. Each older sibling who could help was expected do so, as possible. So they had a formal plan regarding helping one another.

When it became clear our family was in trouble because my dad wouldn't be around to work, Mom's family united in a spirit of helping. Seven of her relatives, including her brothers and sister sent ten dollars a month to help us. That came to a total of seventy dollars a month. Back then ten dollars was a lot of money for somebody to give up. The average income of people in the United States at that time was only about three thousand dollars a year. That means a lot of people were making less than sixty dollars a week. Yet my mom's family was willing to keep us afloat with seventy dollars per month.

FOUNDATIONS

If it hadn't been for that, I don't know how we could have made it. Still, almost everything we had was repossessed. That was before the days when women and children in those kinds of situations could get help from agencies and the government like they can today.

To show you how tough things were, Spiegel's, the mail order catalogue, even sent someone out to repossess our lawnmower. It was Christmastime and the guy was also employed as a department store Santa. That's who came to repossess our lawnmower, Santa Claus. We owed five dollars on it and they had the nerve to repossess it because my mom didn't have the five dollars to pay them.

Unfortunately, my dad's nervous breakdown wasn't the first bad thing to befall my mom. She and her family had actually seen a lot of tragedy. Her dad, my maternal grandfather, died of a heart attack when she was very young. Then they had a fire that burned down the family house. They also lost the cotton business they had. Her mother, my maternal grandmother, had nine kids to feed and clothe.

They all moved to Austin where my grandmother opened a boarding house. One thing you had to say about my mom's family is that instead of letting adversity tear them apart, each bad thing that happened brought them closer together. That's where they got the idea to help each other out financially so as many as wanted could attend college.

Even with everything going on regarding my dad's nervous breakdown and PTSD, God helped us through those times. One of my uncles, Andy Moore, was a veterinarian. He had a two-bedroom house in Hamilton, Texas, where we stayed for a while. Otherwise, we would have been homeless. It was a little house, so what did Uncle Andy do? He moved a bed into his clinic, along with a box fan, and stayed there. That was a really thoughtful thing to do and it required a lot of sacrifice on his part.

When it became apparent we were going to have to stay with family or be homeless, Uncle Andy showed up in a cattle truck. He used it to load up all our things and move us to Hamilton. Uncle Andy was a bachelor and a good old boy. He tried to clean out the cattle truck before loading our furniture, but there was still kind of a mess. You can imagine how the thing looked and smelled. All of the furniture my mother had was put in the back. My mother felt humiliated.

Another setback was getting word that after six months in the veteran's hospital, my dad was still seriously ill. So six months turned into a year. It was a long and difficult twelve months, but mom refused to give up hope. She tried so hard to shield us from how grim things were. She also tried to make sure we had something nice. One way she did that was by literally saving every single penny that was extra. Then, once a week she would buy us an ice cream cone. That was a real luxury and we spent the entire week looking forward to that ice cream cone.

Those experiences brought us together and taught us to pray. I remember this one time when it seemed like everything was going wrong. The weather had turned dark and stormy and there was lightning and thunder everywhere. On top of that, there was a report on the radio that the great evangelist Billy Graham was holding a crusade in another country, but had fallen ill. The news reports said he might even die.

Mother told us he was a great man of God and that we should pray for him. We also prayed for my father's mental health and to be delivered through the storm. It was a fearful thing to talk to God during the middle of a storm with all the lightning and thunder. The lights went out and the wind blew. God seemed fearful, scary, and awesome. However, He answered our prayers. Billy Graham was restored to physical health. My father was eventually restored to mental health. I think that was my first experience in prayer.

I don't mind telling you that early in my childhood I had some mixed emotions about God. He was there during crisis times, like with my dad and Billy Graham. The storm imprinted on my mind that God was also awesome and someone of whom you should be afraid.

While we were living in Hamilton, I began first grade. My entry into school was delayed a year because my birthday was two days after school started. I was made to wait a whole year to enter, so I was a year older than the other children. That didn't seem to matter to me. I was afraid to be away from my mom. I even ran away from school the first day and hid under a tree.

My teachers found me a few hours later; or maybe it was a few minutes. It seemed like hours to me. They brought me back to class, called my mom, and she came up to the school to encourage me. I got over my fear and began to like school. It provided friends and the opportunity to learn new things. I did well in that first year of elementary school in Hamilton. Things were actually looking up.

Chapter 4

DAD STARTS ALL OVER

Randy

It was a year later that my father was released from the hospital. He said he wanted to make a new start. He went to stay with a sister in Weatherford, outside of Fort Worth, because there weren't any engineering jobs in Hamilton. He would commute into Fort Worth with Uncle Ben, who worked there. While Ben was at work, my dad would go around and apply for jobs.

Dad eventually got hired by American Manufacturing. I remember how excited we were when he called and said he found a good position as an engineer. That was the company I told you about in chapter one. As I said, they made large pumps for oil fields.

They had a military side, too. The government would give them an order to make shells for the Navy to use in practice drills. During World War II, they made bombs and shell casings. In square footage, I believe American Manufacturing and General Dynamics were the two largest plants in Fort Worth at that time.

After a couple of paychecks, Dad also found a house for us near Carswell Air Force Base in an area known as Bucko Estates. He sent for us and that's where we moved. We lived near the Air Force base's runway. Carswell was known for the B-36 Peacemaker and

B-58 Hustler. They were both huge bombers. Uncle Ben worked on the B-58, which was the first supersonic delta wing strategic bomber.

The school I attended was also very close by. Our house and the school both shook every time jets took off or landed. But, I had my dad back and our family was all together, so as far as I was concerned, those were good years.

During the Vietnam War, American Manufacturing made five hundred pound bombs. As you can imagine, it took huge equipment to make them, including some thousand ton presses that measured five stories tall. In addition to his other duties, Dad got to help design the new buildings that would house all the presses and furnaces used to make the bombs.

Unfortunately, his year in the hospital hadn't quelled Dad's desire to drink. In spite of that, he was trying to build his relationship with his family and make up for lost time. Looking back, I'm pretty sure the alcohol was a way of self-medicating to deal with his stress. It also wasn't long before the same old symptoms of PTSD resurfaced. Although I loved my dad and admired his engineering abilities, I lost respect for him because of the heavy drinking.

One time, when I was in elementary school, Dad took me with him to a bar he liked. I think it was called the Talley Ho Inn. The centerpiece of the bar was a table game where you slid heavy, flat weights down the table to knock over miniature bowling pins. I still remember how happy I was as a little boy when I succeeded at that game. It made my father proud of me.

My dad had a very nice smile, but his drinking would get him into trouble. His nice smile was "adjusted" during a bar brawl. One of his front teeth was knocked out. That was so hard for my mother. Think about it from her perspective. She had to scrape by while my dad was in the hospital. Then he takes his family to a city where they don't know anyone. But that's okay because her husband is back and he's got a very good engineering job. Then he starts drinking again. He's taking his son to bars with him. And now, to top it all off, he gets a tooth knocked out in a bar fight.

Looking back, things like that really caused the stress to build between him and my mom. But there were some really good things about my dad. My relationship with him tended to still revolve around mechanical things. My dad loved math and he loved the fact I was turning into an engineering type like him. I learned the scientific method from him. He also helped me look at the big picture when it came to problem solving.

He would let me help him fix things, including the family automobile. He enjoyed showing me how to change sparkplugs and brakes and tune up the car. One day we were doing something with an old Mercury. I was leaning over the front fender with my head and upper body over the engine. My feet were on the bumper. It was a windy day and my father went into the garage to get some tools. While he was in the garage, a huge gust of wind came and slammed that long, heavy car hood on top of me. I thought I was going to be cut in half! Of course, I couldn't get out and I could barely breathe with that car hood on me. It was a scary few minutes as I screamed for someone to help me. My father came and lifted the hood. Luckily, there were no broken bones or permanent injuries. I know it scared me to death, but I think it might have scared my dad even more.

Another time, my father was working in the garage. There was a ladder leading up to the attic and Dad was on it doing something. He fell off and broke his wrist. Up to that point, I had seen my dad act irrational. I had seen him act crazy and depressed and delusional and paranoid. But I had never seen my dad physically injured. He was in really bad physical pain. That experience really shook me up.

It happened late at night. Mother put us all in the car and drove us to the hospital. In the emergency room, they set Dad's wrist and put it in a cast. For me as a little boy, there were mixed feelings about what I had seen. My father was brave, yet vulnerable. I wondered if he would be all right. These are pretty normal feelings when your father, somebody you want to be your mentor, is hurt and there's nothing you can do to help.

Despite the knocked-out tooth and the broken wrist, Dad managed earn respect and advance at American Manufacturing. In fact, his brilliance as an engineer was able to shine through. He was even able to invent a few things that directly benefited the company. When the chief engineer retired, my father was promoted to that position, even though he had only been with the company for two years.

Dad ended up staying with American Manufacturing for twenty-six years. His name even appeared on several patents owned by the company for things he invented. For example, he developed a technique making it possible to pump oil from twice the previous depth limit. This opened up a lot of new possibilities for oil companies. Some of those designs are still used in oil fields all over the world. Because he worked for American Manufacturing, they got the money and the credit, but he had the satisfaction of his name being on the patents.

His job success and promotion made it possible for us to buy a house on the other side of town. After two years of living right beside the Air Force base, Dad moved us to an eastside suburb called Haltom City. The house we moved into is still in the family to this very day. I was in third grade at the time. It was really late in the year, but instead of letting me finish the year where I was, I was pulled out and put into this school in Haltom City.

My teacher at the Fort Worth school had been really nice. However, the teacher in Haltom City was really cold and indifferent. That was a new experience for me. I thought all teachers were nice, but that teacher made me realize it wasn't true. Needless to say, I didn't really enjoy the rest of that year of school.

I mentioned earlier that my dad and I really bonded over mechanical things, especially cars. One time we were visiting my granddad, who we called "Big Dad." He lived near Dublin, Texas, and he had this old 1937 LaSalle two-door coupe. Those beauties were famous for having a great engine and transmission, and they went very fast. My dad told me that one day we would fix up that old car and do a complete restoration. Unfortunately, Big Dad didn't remember, or didn't get the message, or something. He sold that car to a passing junk collector. Here was one more disappointment for my dad; something he really cared about that didn't work out right.

On a more positive note, it was that same year that I fell in love for the first time. Her name was Miss Fincannon and she was my fourth grade teacher. She was beautiful. And she seemed to take an interest in me. That was a really good year.

Fourth grade was also the year I began to read Tom Swift adventure stories. They were books about a boy involved in inventing things and having all these science fiction adventures. He had fantastic submarines, ships, and airplanes. There was a good detective angle to the stories, too. I began to stay up late at night reading those books and would sometimes read half a book in an evening. Books became a good escape from some of the things going on with my dad.

When I wasn't traveling with Tom Swift, I was traveling the neighborhood on my bike. One Saturday morning I was riding

36

bikes with one or two friends. We got the idea it would be fun to go see Miss Fincannon. She was very kind and invited us in to have some muffins. We talked and as we did, she told us she was preparing to marry. That bit of news came as a horrible shock.

I just knew she would wait for me to grow up and then be mine. I even cried on the way home. That was my first disappointment in love. I've even blocked out what her married name was. To me she will always be the single woman who taught my class and gave me muffins. To me she will always be Miss Fincannon.

Between Miss Fincannon and Tom Swift, my mind was being stimulated academically. I enjoyed reading and studying. The attention and affirmation of my teacher really aided that process. It's important to have someone who believes in you and says so.

In other relationships I was shy and quiet. Competition was never my strong suit and I didn't like athletics too much. I'm not sure if it came from a lack of experience with sports or a feeling of physical weakness or what the problem was. However, in elementary and junior high school, I would do almost anything to get out of having to compete. I was afraid I would miss the ball and be embarrassed. I was the one who was always picked last when they chose teams. That's not very good for a person's self- image.

My little brother, Rex, was four years younger than me. He was a fat and happy child with a round face. I was tall and skinny. My little sister Nancy was two years younger than Rex. She had blonde hair and was very slender. Like all kids, we would play for hours, building things, digging "caves" in our back yard, climbing trees.

One summer day my brother and I were playing outside and he crawled under the house. The house was pier and beam construction and Rex was peeking out through a grate. I was mad at him about something and got a handful of sand. I threw it at him through the grating and it got in his eyes. He couldn't see, so I had to crawl under the house to help him out. We called for mother and she came and rinsed the sand out of his eyes. I said earlier I didn't like to see people or animals hurt. It bothered me a lot I had hurt someone else intentionally. Talk about guilt.

Even though my mom wasn't attending church during that period, she always emphasized the importance of God in our lives and the power of prayer. The sand incident helped me realize that even though I was a "good person," I still did bad things. That realization did a lot to prepare me for the message of Jesus Christ and my need for forgiveness of my sins.

A church not far from our house was having Vacation Bible School during that period. To publicize the VBS and get neighborhood kids to come, they held a big parade with balloons and horns honking and the whole thing. It really looked like fun. I said, "Mom, can we go?" She said okay and that's how we started attending church.

During those years, we attended a Sunday school and I learned stories from the Bible. Eventually, my mom started attending, as well. I was learning about Jesus, but I still didn't know Him personally. It wasn't our family tradition to stay for church worship services. We would go to the Sunday school and then head home.

Since we didn't stay for services, I don't remember ever hearing anybody extend an invitation to accept Jesus as my personal Lord and Savior. Then one day the pastor of the church came to visit our home. I was eleven at the time. The Sunday school teacher came with him. They explained the good news of Jesus to me, and that He came to forgive our sins and to make us right with God.

As I said, experiences like throwing sand in my brother's eyes showed me I was a sinner, a person who did bad things. I knew I wanted to be forgiven. I prayed to receive Christ that day. I asked the Lord to forgive my sins. I invited Jesus into my heart to be with me forever.

When the pastor and Sunday school teacher left, I knew beyond any shadow of a doubt I was a Christian. I was someone who knew Jesus Christ. That is different from knowing about Him. It's like the difference in knowing about a great person and being personal friends with him. That's all the difference in the world. It was amazing to realize that Jesus Christ wanted to have a personal relationship with me. He had done everything and all I had to do was put my faith in Him. I began to understand I could pray and talk to Him and He would listen.

I was so happy that I went out into the yard and was running and jumping and yelling for joy. My guilt as a sinful person was removed. My soul was secure. I felt confident God would be with me, regardless of what the future would bring. To this day, I believe that experience as an eleven-year-old was the most important thing I've ever done in my life.

It took me over a year to make public my decision to follow Christ and accept His forgiveness. When I did, it was on a Sunday night. It was my first time to attend the service, as opposed to Sunday school. I went forward to make what is called a public profession of faith. That just means I was saying in public what had happened in the privacy of my own heart. I was baptized the very same night.

Church became more important to me and we started to attend more regularly. I started to develop friends at church. One Saturday the Sunday school teacher, along with the leader of the Royal Ambassadors, a club for boys, took us on a field trip. We were going to the county jail! They wanted us to see the people there and talk to us about how everyone needs Jesus. I had never seen men locked up in cells. As we went through the jail, I looked into some of the men's faces. Some were lying in their own vomit in the drunk tank. Others were trying to reach out and grab us through the bars. Others sat staring at us with the coldest, cruelest eyes I've ever seen.

As a young boy, it was a significant thing to be confronted with the difference between good and evil, following the rules and breaking the rules. A crystal-clear memory is etched in my mind of silently praying, "God, help me to not get into trouble. Help me to do right." That trip to the jail made a big impression on me.

One boy who didn't go with us that day was Buster. He was appropriately named because he broke everything, including the rules. Buster was a friend of mine. As he got older, he became more and more rebellious. By the time we were thirteen, he was attending wild parties with older boys and hanging out with kids who were skipping school.

As we got older, Buster and I had less and less in common, which made me sad. He was a really likable person. However, there was little doubt his behavior was going to get him in big trouble one day. By the time I was fifteen, Buster and I didn't really hang out together. But one day I ran into him. He wanted to get me a date with a girl he knew. She lived about twenty miles away.

I had just gotten my driver's license and was talked into borrowing our family car. We picked up the girl, and then he wanted us to go to a party he knew about. Of course, Buster and this girl were just using me, and the fact I had my driver's license, to get a ride to the party.

The girl actually liked an older boy who was already at the party. In a few minutes they were going off to one of the bedrooms of the house so they could be alone. When I went to find them and make sure she was all right, they were in bed together. I left feeling used and hurt about the whole situation.

Later there was another experience with Buster that broke the relationship completely. He invited me to another party with a lot of older teenagers. One older guy was named Floyd. He was known for two things: getting drunk and picking on younger kids. Floyd was getting pretty wasted that night. I was standing around not knowing what to do. I chose to attend the party because I wanted to be friends with Buster. As Floyd got more and more drunk, things got more and more uncomfortable.

At one point I began talking to a girl. She was just someone who was friendly and willing to talk to me. Big mistake. It turned out the girl was with Floyd. At that time, Floyd was in another room telling dirty jokes, laughing, and getting more intoxicated. When he came back in the room where we were, he saw me talking to his girlfriend and immediately threatened to kill me.

It wasn't just an idle threat, either. Floyd pulled out a knife and held me against the wall with the knife to my throat. There was nothing I could do except be scared. I stayed very still and said, "Floyd, I didn't do anything. I didn't know this girl was with you. We were just talking."

Buster and some other fellows came out of the kitchen and took the knife away from Floyd. I was told, "You better get out of here." I had already made the decision that "out of there" was exactly where I needed to be. I got in my car and took off. I never went back to that kind of party ever again.

On a more positive note, I joined a bigger church during my teenage years. It was Oak Knoll Baptist, where they had a large youth group. I have to admit, there were some very pretty girls in the youth group and that didn't hurt things. It was there I met Pastor Jarvis A. Philpot.

Pastor Philpot could really preach. He told dramatic stories that made the Bible come alive. He spoke with authority, too.

There was a lot of enthusiasm in his preaching. It made me love to attend church. I wanted to be part of the youth choir they had, but I lacked confidence in my ability to sing. Eventually I joined, but at first I would just mouth the words.

Regardless of how shy I was, God and Pastor Philpot were helping me become a leader. I was invited to be president of the youth Sunday school, but was too shy to accept. Later, in another year or so, I was asked to be president of the youth choir. This time I accepted. I would lead the choir in prayer and try to bring a spiritual dimension to the choir rehearsals.

In spite of my growing involvement, my father wasn't interested in church. However, he was a big believer in the American work ethic. From the time I was a child, he had emphasized the importance of working hard.

I got my first job when I was just thirteen. It was at a Gulf service station. Dad was proud of me for getting it. I was so excited to be hired that I don't think I even asked what my responsibilities would be. When I realized what was involved, I suddenly felt humiliated. They wanted me to clean the filthy gas station bathrooms. Those bathrooms hadn't been cleaned in months, maybe years. They were a disaster. Feelings of anger, disappointment, and embarrassment swept over me.

Nonetheless, I grabbed buckets, hoses, and mops and confronted the filthy toilets. I was armed with every cleaner I could find in that gas station. Working out of a mixture of anger and wanting to impress the man who gave me the job, I started cleaning. When I finished, the bathrooms were sparkling clean from top to bottom.

Doing a good job on such a lowly task had an interesting result. I earned the boss's respect. A customer came in right after I finished cleaning and said they were the cleanest bathrooms he had ever seen. He even wrote a letter to the local division of Gulf Oil bragging about them. He wrote that these were the best maintained bathrooms he had ever seen in his life.

My good work ethic eventually helped me get a job at a competing station down the street for more money. I was now making sixty-five cents an hour. Then I got an even better job at another station with another pay raise. I was now up to seventy-five cents an hour.

Even though it wasn't much money, I saved it up and bought a 1957 Ford. It was an ex-police car that had been wrecked. It was all worn out, but I was proud to have it. I invested all my spare time the next two years fixing it up.

In the cool of the evenings in our neighborhood, people would sit outside and visit. One man I visited with was Jack Baker. He was a foreman at a small construction company that built sidewalks, patios, and swimming pools. He could tell I was interested in mechanical things and invited me to apply for a job with his company. I applied and was hired as his helper. Jack taught me how to shovel sand and gravel, make cement and sand-blast buildings. I also learned all kinds of repair techniques.

I landed that job when I was fifteen. By the time I was sixteen, I found they needed a truck driver, so I applied. I got my truck driving license and drove some of the trucks. Being mechanically minded, thanks to my dad, I was also able to work on things and fix them. That increased my value as an employee.

Dad really wanted all us kids to understand the American work ethic. That was his religion. Even when we did jobs around the house, he would pay us for them. All that work, along with a growing sense of who I was in the Lord, gave me improved confidence. I went from being a kid who was afraid to compete to the chin-up champion of Carter Riverside High School. Nobody could beat me at chin-ups.

By the time I was seventeen, my father had seen enough to know I was a really good employee. He was the one who offered me a job at the factory. My title would be Electrician's Assistant. I was introduced to George Haas, the man I would be helping. As I said earlier, American Manufacturing was in need of employees so they could crank out the products to meet multiple oil companies and Defense Department contracts.

But the company was expanding so fast that they had really inexperienced people in supervisory positions. Someone might do a pretty good job managing a few men or a small department. But that didn't mean they were the right person to manage many people and huge departments.

Suddenly, there were hundreds of new employees working seventy and eighty hours a week to keep up with the demand. The management of the company was quite brutal. There were no unions, no company benefits, and no insurance. People were told they were lucky to have a job and they were supposed to do what they were told. That was all.

Some of the truck drivers tried to unionize for better working conditions and benefits. The company bosses had them line up in the parking lot and fired them in front of everyone. Those who wanted a job learned not to say anything, no matter how bad things got. The company safety rules were inadequate. Even the few rules they had were ignored, especially by the bosses.

One time they were lifting some transformers over power lines. The plan was to drop them down into another bank of transformers. As they were backing up the crane, it sank into some soft earth. That caused the crane's boom to hit a thirteen thousand volt power line. It killed a worker on the ground who was touching the truck. Why did that happen? Because they wouldn't turn off the electricity to the factory for even a few minutes. That might slow down production.

Another time men were working on the compressors. There was a need to clean around the fly wheel and belts. The foreman, Sam, wouldn't let them turn things off. He told the guy to just clean it while it was running. The guy slipped and was killed. It was very dangerous, but there weren't the kinds of safety rules there are today. When people ask why there are so many rules to follow from the Occupational Safety and Health Administration, or OSHA, it's because things like this used to happen all the time. Before there were all the rules, when a bad accident happened, companies just swept it under the rug. Nobody ever made things safer because they didn't have to.

Chapter 5

FATIGUE

Randy

Looking back, I really believe a large part of what contributed to the accident that killed George Haas and took my arms was fatigue. The men at that plant were working seven days a week in shifts often lasting more than ten hours. People went for months without a day off. With the heat and humidity you often get in Texas, it was brutal. After doing this, going months without a day off and working such long shifts, people began to make mistakes.

Besides, as I said, people were promoted to positions and supervising numbers of people in ways they just weren't trained to handle. The simple rules a company might have developed to run a machine shop with thirty employees just weren't adequate to handle the kind of things going on at the factory, especially as it continued to grow to thousands of employees.

The factory also lacked a master plan for development. As the company grew, they would just add a new building or run more wiring. Nobody was making sure it all fit together in a way that made long-term sense and was truly safe. When they needed more power, they would just add a new line. Further, there was no standard way for powering up and down the areas where people were working.

There were thousands of employees working as fast and hard as they could seven days a week. Then you had people who were in supervisory roles who had no business with that kind of authority. Added to that, no one was really inspecting or making sure things were really safe. It was a recipe for disaster.

That kind of stress really takes its toll on people. My dad would put away a six-pack of beer or more each night. Mom would fix a meal, but he would say no, he didn't want to eat. Actually, he was living on barbecue sandwiches from a place called Sammy's. He loved them. He also loved going out and drinking.

He would come home from work, drink beer, and then go back to the factory and work more, grabbing a barbecue sandwich on the way. His way of dealing with stress was beer and barbecue. He also liked to smoke. From the time he was thirteen, he chain-smoked two packs of unfiltered Camel cigarettes a day.

The same Sunday morning George and I were working on the roof, the foreman called in a buddy of his who was a high voltage electrical contractor. They were working from a truck. Meanwhile, we were working up on the roof. When they were through with their work, the electricity was simply turned back on. It wasn't possible to prove exactly who did it because everybody was blaming each other.

At that time, it was almost impossible to sue an employer if you got injured. The injured person had to prove there was intent to injure. Besides, if we did sue, Dad would have lost his job. Back in that time, seeking damages because of gross negligence wasn't possible.

Thinking back on the days right before my accident, I can tell you in spite of how potentially dangerous the job was, I really liked working at the factory. It was a great experience and I was doing important work. However, I didn't like working on Sunday.

Going to church, along with telling people about Jesus, were the most important things in my life. I wanted to go to church so I could continue to learn and to grow in the Lord. At sixteen I made a really deep commitment to the Lord. I wanted to serve Him every way I could and tell everyone I knew about Him. I guess I was an emerging leader in our youth group. Pastor Philpot said so, anyway. There were some deacons in the church who took me under their wing since my dad didn't go to church and didn't really care about Christianity. They were J.R. Tillery and Clyde Gagster. I really owe them a huge debt of gratitude. They were my surrogate spiritual fathers, mentoring me in living out the Word of the Lord.

So off I went to the factory, after having my pancakes and cleaning up. A bit later that morning, my dad got up and decided he needed to go into the factory, too. Later my mother told me that Dad wanted to go make sure all the power was off. She thought maybe Dad had a premonition something bad was about to happen. He had just gotten to his office when suddenly the lights all dimmed. It was like one of those scenes out of the old gangster movies where all the lights dim when the switch is thrown as they electrocute the prisoner. A minute or two later, somebody called and told my dad what happened.

When my mom got to the hospital after the accident, they wouldn't let her in to see me. I was told later that both she and my dad could see me through the windows lying on a stretcher shaking. The condition she saw me in was hideous, like something out of a horror movie. My mom said she could see me going into convulsions. They also had to perform an emergency tracheotomy. Then they let my parents in for a few minutes.

FATIGUE

George Haas, the man I was working with who was killed, had taken a bit of well-earned time off just prior to the accident. His vacation was over on Friday and he would have normally started back to work that next Monday. But, like me, he was asked to come in on Sunday. So when he left his family that Sunday morning, it was the last time they would ever see him alive.

At the time of the accident, we were both up on a tower. I was down about seven feet below George on the platform. I was handing George a pair of pliers. That was the moment the power was turned on. It seems like the electricity went through George and into me. My mom said it even knocked out the fillings in my teeth. I was spitting them out for days.

I'm told Pastor Philpot was right in the middle of his sermon when the message got to him about the accident. He stopped preaching, said a prayer, and dismissed everyone. They began to hurry to the hospital to pray for me.

The question on everyone's mind was would I live, and if so, for how long?

Chapter 6

THE WORLD IS A DANGEROUS PLACE

Randy

As you can imagine, my parents were devastated. Pastor Philpot spread the word and people poured into the hospital. I'm grateful for their prayers and that God allowed me to live. But even though the amputations helped me through the critical phase, I wasn't anywhere close to being done with this awfulness.

I spent the next year and a half in and out of the hospital. There were thirty-eight surgeries. That averages out to almost two per month. Anyone who has had one surgery, and I mean the old-fashioned kind where they fully cut you open to operate, knows how long it takes to recuperate. I had to trust the Lord for each and every breath through it all. And then there were incidents like the one I told you about earlier with the routine surgery on an otherwise healthy eighteen-year-old. He died and people wondered if it was because he was given just a little too much anesthesia. I literally never knew if I would come through each surgery. But Pastor Philpot always reminded me to put my confidence in the Lord because He could bring me through.

THE WORLD IS A DANGEROUS PLACE

I'd like to say my faith was so strong I could just relax and give myself completely to God's plan. The truth is that each and every operation was a mingling of fear and belief. Ultimately, I had to trust God to intervene and keep me alive.

The surgeries were arduous. I had always been really slender, weighing only one hundred and twenty-five pounds before the accident. Three months after the accident, I was down to eighty-nine pounds. At six feet tall, I looked like a starvation victim or someone from Auschwitz.

Fifty-five percent of my body was covered with third degree burns. The doctors had to take healthy skin from places that weren't burned and put them on places that were. That meant they had to scrape the top layer of skin from my legs to cover my back and sides. That left me with huge open wounds, not only where I was burned, but on the non-burned areas from my hips to my ankles. These are what burn specialists call "donor sites."

That resulted in great pain, even in the places that weren't burned because they scraped such large amounts of skin off them. The pain was continuous. Eventually, though, they took enough skin from unburned areas to cover all the burned ones.

After that, the next step in recuperation was the process to rebuild my left arm. That would involve a twelve-hour surgery. However, there were several other plastic surgeries first. I mentioned the fact they had to cover the open holes with thin skin from my legs. Well, that wasn't sufficient to support a tendon graph to hook my elbow back up.

For that, the surgeons needed full-thickness skin. They created what is called a pedicle flap. It was put on my side and it worked like a trap door. It was lifted; they cut the thin skin graph off, patched the hole with another graph from my leg three inches by five inches, and sewed the arm that was left from my remaining limb to my stomach for three months.

Once Dr. Gracia was sure there were enough blood vessels from the arm to the flap, he cut the flap off and freed it up, but it took several months to be sure it would work. Then they did another twelve-hour surgery with a bone surgeon. Dr. Jack West drilled a hole through one of the upper bones in the left lower arm. He took the myelin sheath off one of the muscles in my leg just above my knee. He rolled it up and made a cord out of it. Then he attached one end of the cord to the burnt end of the bicep muscle, came down through the bone and back to the bicep muscle. It was kind of a pulley system. If it worked I would have use of my remaining elbow. It took several months for the graft to heal. However, during the process, scar tissue formed inside my elbow joint. This caused it to lock up and be unable to flex. Months later it would take another surgery to break it loose. After the surgery it took six months of therapy to get my elbow flection back to ninety degrees of motion.

Every month the pain was getting less, but that's a relative term, as you can imagine. The thing that kept me alive, and I cannot say enough about this, was the loving attitude of my mother. She basically lived in the hospital with me and encouraged me night and day. She would say over and over, "God has something special for you. Otherwise He wouldn't have kept you alive. You are going to have a great life."

She would also say, "I know it hurts right now, but it won't always feel like this." That was so comforting and healing and helpful. I still find great strength in those words. It recognizes the reality of the pain, but it also points to the hope of a better tomorrow.

Also vitally important were the visits by Pastor Philpot. Many times he came to see me twice a day, but always at least once a day at bedtime. He came to encourage me and to pray with me.

He would pray me to sleep and sometimes it was midnight or one in the morning before he left. Keep in mind he had his job pastoring Oak Knoll Church and had to be there at eight the next morning. He was under the tremendous pressure pastors are constantly facing. In spite of all that, he came every single night. What an amazing man of God. He lived out everything the Bible taught about compassion and going the extra mile.

Uncle Ben was another great source of strength. One night I was having a spiritual crisis. I kept asking God why this had to happen to me. I said, "I was trying to live for Jesus, so why me?"

At that time, Uncle Ben was visiting and I asked everyone else to leave the room. I asked Uncle Ben if God was punishing me for the sin in my life. "Did I do something wrong, something evil?"

Uncle Ben paused for a long time and then said, "God don't torture His children; He loves them. If He punished us for every sin, there wouldn't be one of us left alive. God loves us."

Then he explained, "The world is a dangerous place. That's just a fact. But in spite of that, if we call out to God, He will always bring some good out of terrible situations." I took that as Gospel Truth and I still believe it today. In fact, in spite of everything that was happening, Uncle Ben was bold in proclaiming to anyone who would listen, "I still believe in a God of Miracles."

Somebody reading this book may need to hear this, so let me be clear. The search for why bad things happen to good people has continued for years. It will probably continue for many more. But Uncle Ben was right. The world is a dangerous place. But God is good. God loves us. When bad things happen, we can run from God or we can run to Him. If something happens and a human being with a free will did it, whether on purpose or by accident, why do we blame God? God is good. Uncle Ben pointed that out and it settled things for me.

Even though the physical pain from the burns and surgeries were getting better, the random firings of the severed nerves created pain that flashed back to the original accident. I began to get attacks of what's called phantom pain, along with twitching nerves. The doctors explained it this way: When you sever a major nerve, the brain no longer receives accurate signals from the limb. When stimulated, the nerve replays the last message it received. In my case, it was being set on fire. It felt like hot knives cutting into my shoulders. I would bang my shoulders against the wall to change the pain or stop the nerves from firing randomly.

What was the last thing my brain knew regarding those nerves? Almost being burned to death. That cycle of signals kept firing endlessly. Pain medicine won't stop that kind of pain because it is false signals from damaged nerves sending false information. Although it's incorrect information, it feels completely real.

Being around people was difficult because I was acutely aware of my missing limbs. Even well-meaning people would stare and their children would shrink back. Going out was an emotional ordeal that triggered new cycles of phantom pain. One evening some close friends stumbled onto a brilliant idea. They said, "Why don't we make you some fake arms?" Then people won't notice you're missing your right arm and left hand. It was a simple idea with a profound effect. We all plunged into the project. When the foam rubber arms were finished I was more relaxed around people. We went to the local artificial limb shop and bought a right and left rubber glove that looked very much like real hands. They looked so real that when I was out in public I was not so embarrassed or nervous about my appearance.

I became more relaxed around people. Also, when I looked down, my brain registered arms being there. This seemed to break the cycle of the brain searching for signals from the nerves, and replaying false signals of burning pain. This reduced the phantom pain. Soon I was strong enough to be fitted for functional artificial limbs.

Decades later, a medical researcher created visual representations of missing arms for amputees. The device was called a Mirror Box. It reflected the remaining arm to the other side, changing the visual feedback the brain is getting when you look down toward the missing limb. So now what they did for me decades ago to meet a need has become established therapy to help deal with phantom pain.

The accident had happened in late March of my senior year in high school. I had already earned all the credits I needed to graduate, so the school district just let me forget about that last semester. When graduation came, I was bandaged from my neck to my waist and from my thighs to my ankles. They loaded me in the car and took me to commencement exercises.

Since I was in a wheelchair, they didn't have me sit out with the other students. If I had done that, there wouldn't be any way to get me up on the stage. I was just too weak at that point. So they rolled me back stage where no one could see me until they called my name. When that happened, my dad was supposed to roll me out onto the stage to get my diploma. My name was called, but nothing happened.

My mom and a lot of the family who had come into town were all sitting in the audience waiting, but there was just awkward silence. No Randy. What happened? The wheelchair's wheels became tangled in the light cords running across the stage. My dad couldn't get the wheelchair past them.

After a really long silence, my dad was finally able to get me past all the electrical cords and roll me out. He parked my wheelchair. I stood up and walked the rest of the way with dad beside me. I probably walked a grand total of six feet. It wasn't a very long distance, but it totally exhausted me.

There was a standing ovation because most people didn't think I would survive to see that day. My mom said the ovation literally lasted ten minutes. When the school officials on stage reached out to hand me the diploma, my dad took it on my behalf. I then turned my head toward my dad and he turned the tassel to the other side. When the ceremony was finished a few people came up on stage to congratulate me. Gradually, everyone left to go celebrate. They were going out to dinner with family or friends, or to attend a graduation party. I couldn't go. I had to be on my way back to the hospital to continue the long series of surgeries.

When people go through graduation, they are usually thinking about college, the military, or the world of work. They see their whole life in front of them, all their dreams and plans. All I could think about were more surgeries and more pain. Of course, I was also thinking about the God who would see me through it all.

Chapter 7

HOLY SUFFERING

Randy

By this time the tracheotomy tube had been removed and the hole in my neck was gradually closing. First I could just whisper, then talk a little bit. My number one job most days was trying to gain a little more weight. I had become dangerously thin. The hospital had me eating four meals a day and a milkshake at night to try to gain weight.

Things in the hospital had become pretty lonesome. Some friends joined the military. Others went off to college. But thanks to my mother, Pastor Philpot, and Uncle Ben, I was able to say, "God, take this mess and redeem it for your good." Once I did that, everybody I encountered came away changed. Pastor Philpot said this accident changed a lot of people because of the spirit of holy suffering. People would come into the hospital room when I was there and could feel the Holy Spirit in the room.

When something like this happens, a terrible tragedy, it is vital to say, "God, please bring some good out of this mess." After a while, when someone was near death in the hospital, and no one knew what to say, they would come get me. It would take two strong orderlies to get me out of bed and into a wheelchair. One would get me by my ankles and the other would get me by the back of my neck. They would lift me up, put me into a wheelchair, and bundle me up. Then they would take me to be with the family.

One of the patients near death was Bob, a victim of a gasoline fire. He was charred completely black. He was conscious enough to talk. Dr. Gracia felt he would only live a few hours. They quickly took me down there to talk to him before he died. I was scared to death. I had never seen anyone like that. I just tried to encourage him to seek God. That was the first time I was ever a chaplain, even though I myself was still in bad shape. Later I worried, had I said the right things or not?

Pastor Philpot said it wasn't so much about what I said, whether it was to Bob or someone else. It was about the Holy Spirit being there in the room. When the Holy Spirit is in the room, people, even non-Christians, can feel it.

Bob died a little while later, but before he did, he let me pray with him. I was so thankful that God was able to redeem my situation by letting me be a comfort to another person in pain. There were people I was able to minister to only because we were going through the same things. I knew what they were feeling. Through me, they could see that even severely burned people can be used by God.

That didn't mean I wasn't still experiencing pain. It was still very intense. In the reconstruction process of my left elbow, the plan was to save it so I could wear a prosthetic device that would allow me to drive, write, eat, shave, and dress. The future of all those plans depended on saving the left elbow and getting it working.

To do that required a lengthy tendon graph surgery with a team of specialists. That surgery was successful. After a few weeks, I was able to begin physical therapy. But they still had to do one more surgery to break lose the adhesions. They got the elbow moving, but all these years later, I still only have ninety degrees of motion. A normal elbow would have one hundred and forty-five to one hundred and sixty degrees of motion.

Once, when they did a skin graph on my back, they turned me on my side and used adhesive tape to keep me from moving. They literally taped me to the bed rail. They had water dripping on my back for seventy-two straight hours. They had to keep putting water on it so the skin would begin to heal and grow. But it hurt so bad I was convinced I was dying by the time they cut me lose. At one point I was screaming in pain.

But like I said earlier, this was the 1960s and medical professionals were terrified someone might get addicted to pain medication. My parents finally said, "If he gets addicted, we will deal with that. He has to get through this right now."

When the skin grafts healed and I was well enough to travel, it was time for the next step in my journey. I was going to California to get my first set of artificial arms. Normally, a person would go to a local prosthetics shop close by. For me, that would have meant somewhere in Dallas or Fort Worth Texas. However, my case was really severe and I needed a lot of vocational rehabilitation. There were only three places in the United States that could offer the kind of intense therapy I needed to go along with the new arms. One was in Los Angeles, another was in Chicago, and I think the third was In Houston. However, my doctors thought the best one was the UCLA Medical Center in Los Angeles. So that's where I went.

At that time the company's workman's compensation insurance would only pay two hundred dollars toward the first set of arms; they cost twelve hundred dollars. My mother applied to the Texas Rehabilitation Commission for help. They saw that I was a young man with really good grades and a lot of potential, so they agreed to find me the highest-quality rehabilitation center. They also agreed the best place for my situation was the prosthetic and burn center at UCLA in California.

Workman's Compensation paid for the airfare and my mom and I flew out on American Airlines. It was the first time either one of us had flown on a jet. My mom was an optimist and she was so excited. In fact, she was thrilled. I was out of the hospital and we were going to California. The flight out was interesting. We flew from Love Field in Dallas. But with no arms, there were some very practical issues we needed to address. What would I do when I had to go to the bathroom? This was before the days of handicapped or family bathrooms.

I tried to not drink anything that whole day. By the time we landed in Los Angeles, though, I was just dying to go. We looked around for what to do. There was a young military guy there and I had to ask him, "Man, would you please just pull down my zipper. I'm in real trouble here." Then he zipped it back up after I went. I am forever grateful.

When we left for California, we thought it would just take a week or two. My thinking was, "I'll go out there, get my arms, and then I'll be able to get right to work." Neither my mom nor I had any idea how long it would take or what was involved in learning to use prosthetic arms.

We arrived in California just after Christmas. We stayed in some little apartments with kitchenettes recommended by the UCLA Medical Center. They reminded me of dorm apartments. There was one bedroom and a couch that actually served as a bed. I slept on that and my mom took the bedroom.

This was before the days of people using credit cards. You had to get cash for the trip and then watch your money very carefully. My mom could then turn in the expenses for travel, taxis, and meals to Workman's Comp upon our return. But we had to pay for it all up front. Mom did a great job managing, so I didn't have to worry about it.

When we arrived, one person we met was Margaret Orchard. She was my vocational therapist and she was fantastic. She worked with me on strengthening my body. I'd been laying down for a year and a half. I didn't have any way to exercise. And the burns disrupted my body's thermostat. So if I started sweating at all from exertion, it was almost unbearable. I remember that my body's thermostat was so out of whack that, once I got out of the hospital, I'd stand outside on the coldest of winter nights back in Fort Worth with no coat on, trying to cool off.

Margaret did the initial evaluations. She also made several attempts to work with my right shoulder. Unfortunately, the nerves were still so sensitive I couldn't wear any type of prosthetic device. In fact, the nerve damage was so severe she couldn't even touch my right shoulder. She explained that the severed nerves were too close to the surface. It was going to be necessary to open up my most severely damaged side and cut the nerves back to try and reduce the sensitivity.

We kept trying to get it to work so that more surgeries wouldn't be required. However, Margaret and the others at UCLA Medical Center finally said, "We're so sorry. You're going to have to get more surgery. They've got to resection the shoulder and bury those nerves."

My mom was heartbroken. Here was another setback, another two-, three-, or four-month delay. But she was the type who believed in keeping others cheered up. She didn't like to show disappointment. Still, I could tell how hard it was on her. In spite of the setback, we were both committed to keeping our heads up and smiling. We couldn't focus on the disappointment. Our attitude had to be, "Let's look forward to the adventure to come."

My dad had his pressures, too. He was an executive at the company where his son was nearly killed. If he pressed it too much about compensation for the injury, his job would be at stake. The family of George Haas was suing, so the company wondered if they could trust my dad not to also litigate. There was enormous pressure on him every day and probably a lot of intimidation.

I remember people would just flippantly say, "You ought to sue them. Get some money to take care of yourself."

Dad would always respond, "If you ever sue your company, you will never work again. Nobody will ever hire you because they can't trust you." None of us had any idea what kind of money it was going to take for recovery and maintenance, but we knew if my dad lost his job, that would only make things worse.

Dad had always had trouble dealing with stress. Then this happened. That didn't help the marital difficulties he and my mother were having. Then there was the drinking to self-medicate that he had been doing for years. When I think about all the pressure he was under, I actually think he did an amazing job holding it together. There was also the issue of what my arms were going to cost, not just now, but in the future.

Mom and I returned to Fort Worth for the surgery to resection the nerves, burying them deeper in the shoulder. That meant another hospital stay and all the pain that went with it. Through it all, whether I was in California with Mom getting my prosthetic arms or back in Fort Worth, my spiritual support team was right there beside me. Every time I was out of the hospital, Pastor Philpot would come and get me and take me out to do something.

Pastor Philpot had a white Dodge Challenger. It was sporty and had a fastback spoiler on the rear. He was probably in his early thirties at the time, and a sharp dresser. Sometimes, he'd take me to get a hamburger or maybe go to Cox's Department Store to look at suit jackets. I was already shy, but not having any arms, I didn't want to go in any stores. Pastor Philpot would coax me out of the car.

We would go into the department store, walking past the perfume counter and the candy counter. Then we got to the men's clothes. Of course, he would also have to help the clerks get over the shock of seeing me. Pastor Philpot would explain that I was hurt in an accident.After that, they would help me try things on.

The reaction we got most often from people, because they didn't know how to react, was that I became invisible. They ignored me like I wasn't there. They were so afraid of saying or doing the wrong thing that they didn't do anything at all. My advice is when you encounter someone with a handicap, don't make a big deal out of it. Treat them like You would anyone else. If you see they need assistance, say, "Hey, can I give you some help?"

Occasionally, because of my age and the fact the Vietnam War was going on, people would sometimes ask if I got hurt in the war. I would say, "No, it was an industrial accident." But it would start a conversation. I wasn't invisible to those people. That was really important to me. Speaking of the war, remember that there was a draft back then. I had to go before the draft board and prove I had two artificial arms and couldn't serve in the military.

Once I was out of the hospital, mom and I went back out to California two or three months later to try again. This time it was with the realization that none of us had any sort of idea what was going to be involved in the recovery process.

It was spring in Southern California. In spite of all the pain and everything involved, I remember how beautiful it was there and how much my mom enjoyed seeing it. I was going for physical therapy every day for three weeks with Margaret Orchard. Meanwhile the people at UCLA Medical Center fabricated my prosthetic arms.

The arms really hurt at first. I could only wear them for an hour or so. Then I'd rest for two hours before doing it all again. The weight of the contraption all rested right on my shoulder. Because I was naturally skinny and then lost so much weight, it was resting right on the bone, which really hurt. Both prosthetics were made of plastic and fiberglass. A hook on each arm was controlled by cables, which went to straps around my body. Some straps held the arms on. Others pulled the cables to make the hooks and elbow work.

The first set of arms operated very differently from one another. The left arm system was below the elbow. It was pretty light weight. Everything was controlled by cables. It was basically the same thing you would get today if you went in for a simple set of mechanical arms. The right arm system was very heavy and hard to deal with. It hurt to move.

When I put them on, all the straps and buckles had to be very, very tight. Somebody had to do that, usually my mom. Then I'd put on the left arm and try that. It turned out the straps on the left prosthetic device actually helped hold the right one in place. I discovered it was better to wear both, rather than just one. However, I would put them on and after an hour it would hurt so badly, I had to take them off and rest.

A lot of new amputees find this is the case. The skin isn't used to the weight and the pressure. They also find that the skin making contact with the device is still injured and swollen. I had this misconception that I'd just put them on and get on with my life. Reality wasn't that simple.

What you don't realize about prosthetic arms is that every tiny motion has to be practiced over and over and over to learn what needs to be done. Every task was far more difficult than I could have ever dreamed. Trying to pick up a pencil, much less trying to get it in position to write with it, took hours when I first started. Trying to buckle a belt was agonizing. Every day I went to these occupational therapy classes and practiced stacking blocks or trying to write my name.

Pencils or pens or anything with a smooth surface tended to slide right off the metal hooks before I could grip them. I used lots and lots of rubber bands. Later, I learned to slip rubber tubing over one of the hook fingers which helped me get a better grip on whatever I was trying to pick up. But using the rubber bands to make the grip stronger meant it required more force to open the hooks. This hurt my shoulder. It was kind of a vicious cycle. Still, one of the best gifts anybody ever gave me was twenty-five cents worth of rubber tubing to slip on the ends of the hooks so they would grip.

I had to learn to pick up a pen and then adjust it into position to write. But inevitably I would drop it and it rolled across the floor and under something. Then I had to figure out how to get myself and the prosthesis positioned to get under there and retrieve it. If I dropped a car key under the car, I had to figure out how to get under the car to get it. These are things that seem like an inconvenience to a person with arms and hands, but certainly not insurmountable. When you have two prostheses, it can mean thirty or forty-five minutes recovering everything so you can just try to do it again, this time without dropping something.

Fortunately, I'm not a perfectionist. I'm a survivor. So if I dropped something or couldn't get a grip on it and had to start over, I would. I just had to. No two ways about it. Even the simplest things can take hours, especially when you are just learning.

Being born right handed, I had to learn to do everything left handed. So on top of everything else, I was using a hook to learn to write, drive, shave, and eat. I did experiment with writing with my feet, but with very mixed results.

On Mother's Day, 1967, I presented my mom with a card I had tried to sign by holding the pen between my toes. That didn't go so well. The card was presented with a watch on a chain that went around her neck. They were very popular back then and she loved it. I had asked one of the nurses to take some of my money and go and buy the present so I could give it to her. I know she loved the card and the fact I tried to sign it with my feet.

It didn't take long to figure out writing with my feet wasn't for me. It was far more practical to learn to do it with a hook. That took some time. I got my new arm in May of 1967 and worked constantly on using it to write and do other things.

Speaking of writing, this was before the days of the Internet, nationwide unlimited long distance, or any of that. When we were in California, my mom wrote letters every couple of days to my little brother and sister. We would also call every few days. Long distance cost something like fifty cents per minute, so we didn't talk long. We had to go through the operator, as well as the switchboard operator for the little apartment we were staying in near UCLA.

To be honest, my plate was so full with everything that was happening to me, I didn't think a lot about what life was like for my little brother and sister, Rex and Nancy. Long after the accident, Nancy shared with me her perspective on things from a little sister's point of view.

She told me, "I distinctly remember the night before your accident. We had that aquarium we tended. When you came home, you noticed one of our angel fish had died. You tried to resuscitate it by propelling it through the water, trying to force water through its gills, hoping it would survive."

Twenty-four hours later, people were trying to resuscitate me, hoping I would survive. There was a huge emotional toll on Nancy and Rex. They saw me so injured and had no idea if I was going to make it. Nancy told me it was hard because the accident basically left her and Rex without a mother for months and months and months. She wasn't bitter at all, but she was honest about how difficult it was. I really appreciated that.

Nancy said, "Of course, there was a void in our home. Mom stayed with you in the hospital night and day for a very long time. I don't remember Dad being involved that much. I'm sure he was distraught over the accident, but his role just doesn't play much in my memory. It was Mom who was there for everyone. I do remember Mom was not happy with Dad's decision not to sue American Manufacturing. She saw it as choosing the company over his son. But Dad wanted to be sure to keep his position there."

The accident basically left Nancy and Rex without a mother in the home. Nancy said, "The hospital is where I ate dinner every night. It became a second home and the nurses became a part of my life. They were the ones who pierced my ears. The cooks in the coffee shop became like part of our family."

Nancy's best friend Karen lived two houses down from us and Nancy was also able to spend a lot of time there. Rex was older, thirteen and fourteen during this time, and more able to take care of himself. Nancy said, "Rex was the one who suffered the most loneliness since I had my friend Karen." That just shows how these kinds of tragedies can have a far reaching impact in ways you don't even realize at the time. I had my mom. Nancy had Karen. Dad has his work. Rex had no one.

Honestly, though, in 1967, very little of that was on my mind. I was thinking about getting well and getting on with my education and life. I couldn't do that until I learned to use my new arms.

So, with the help of Mom and Margaret Orchard, I kept working to master them.

After a while, I could wear the artificial arms for two hours and rest for one. Finally, I could wear them all day. Since 1967, I have been able to wear the artificial arms for eighteen hours a day. Over the years, I have worn out many sets of arms. If the wind catches a door when I have it in my hook, it can break the hook off. I remember one time I was going for a job interview, opened the door with a hook, the wind caught it and broke the aluminum hook right as I was going in.

Also, where the hook curves is a stress point and they can break there. Doors, car doors, and twisting things open are constantly putting pressure on them. At first, I wore two hooks because I couldn't stand the weight of artificial hands. They tried giving me steel hooks, but those are so heavy I couldn't use them. Therefore, the hooks I finally decided on were aluminum alloy, which isn't as strong, but I could tolerate the weight.

Breaking the hooks isn't just an inconvenience. It's also expensive. When I first got hurt, each hook was fifty-five dollars. That was like a week's pay. You break one; you just lost a week's income.

There are other parts that wear out on prosthetic arms. The wrist unit has a three-position hinge that gets so wallowed out, as we would say in the South, and so loose, you can't get it to stay in place or write with it. When that wrist fails, it's like holding a pen that's broken halfway down and trying to write. In spite of your best efforts, it won't go where you want it to go.

The hook is actually much more usable than an artificial hand, but it freaks people out when they see it, especially when someone is wearing two of them. Little kids run and hide when they see the hooks. I wear the artificial hand on my right side and the hook on the left now. But I wear the hand for other people, not for me.

68

When I was in engineering school in college, I wore two hooks so I could use them to move things around for my drafting class. In fact, I wore two hooks the first five years. I got the artificial hand on my right side toward the end of university. I couldn't use it as well and sometimes, because I carried a heavy briefcase, it would even break the fingers.

The summer of '67 has been called the Summer of Love. The Beatles came out with their *Sgt. Pepper's Lonely Hearts Club Band* album. The anti-war movement and "Give Peace a Chance" were very much a part of the youth culture. Thousands of young people were converging on the Haight Ashbury section of San Francisco. Styles were changing. Long hair for boys was popular and the word *hippie* had entered everyone's vocabulary.

What was foremost on my mind in the summer of '67 was that I had become comfortable enough with my prosthetic arms and the hooks that I wanted to try and rejoin the world. That was the summer I went back to work. That meant returning to the place where the accident happened.

Chapter 8

FORGIVING SAM

Randy

The factory where my dad and I worked had a policy that if you got injured on the job, you could come back after you recuperated. They would do their best to try to find some position for you, maybe in another area. They didn't have any disability insurance, so that was their only plan for people who got hurt on the job.

Since my dad worked in the engineering department, they arranged for me to be a draftsman. That also fit with the fact I wanted to be an engineer one day. In spite of the accident, I still planned to start college soon and major in engineering. I knew engineering was primarily a science of the mind. Even if I didn't have arms, I could still invent. I could still find ways to design machines.

I worked that summer to learn to use my hooks and do simple drafting. Getting back to work was therapy. I was in the engineering department now, instead of the electrical department. While I was learning to use my hooks, I was modifying the drawings and then carrying them to the shop to be built. They were the size of a table, but they folded to the size of a piece of notebook paper.

I could clip them to a clipboard and carry them that way. Walking from the office to the factory was good exercise for me.

The job forced me out of the house. I could also go to lunch with other people. But I tried to never go back to the part of the factory where I was injured. That would bring back too many horrible memories. At the same time, I was set on overcoming this tragedy and not letting it get the best of me.

One day I bumped into Sam, the foreman who had ordered the electricity turned back on. He never did tell me he was sorry. He never even said he was sorry the accident happened. For five years I had to look him in the face any time I encountered him. He had this really hard exterior. In fact, it seemed to me he was as hard as the machines they were using to make shells, casings, and oilfield equipment.

And though I saw him relatively often, I really can't tell you what he was like. He never let anybody see any part of him except that hard shell. Sam wasn't careful with people's lives. As I said earlier, George Haas wasn't the only person killed working at that factory.

When it came to the accident that killed George and injured me, my parents said a lot of the records regarding the accident and what happened that day disappeared. They were either destroyed by the company or somebody walked off with them so they couldn't be found. We really don't know whether it was a cover-up or just more incompetence due to the speed at which the factory had grown.

One thing I had to work through was the struggle of forgiving someone who didn't accept any responsibility and who didn't go away. I had to see him over and over, knowing he was not repentant. I forgave him in my heart. It was important to do that so the seed of bitterness didn't take root and destroy my life.

When did that actually happen? When did I forgive Sam and not just think about needing to forgive him? It happened during one of my prayer times. It might have been four years after the accident. I was doing homework from college. I had to ask myself, do I sit here and be bitter or do I get on with my life? Forgiving someone is such a relief because it allows you to have that burden of bitterness lifted off your shoulders. And believe me, my shoulders didn't need any more weight on them. The artificial arms were quite enough.

As far as any legal fallout from the accident, we never could get to the bottom of anything. Everybody blamed everybody else. And Sam wouldn't talk about it. A lawyer in Fort Worth told my mom he could pursue it and get a large settlement. That was just talk because nothing ever came of it. Even he couldn't get anybody to say anything. People just talked in circles and waited for it to go away.

My mother also had to deal with forgiveness. One of the hardest things for her was forgiving herself. She later said that, when she got news of the accident, she immediately thought the whole thing was her fault. The idea hit her hard, making her feel that the accident happened because God was punishing us. She felt guilty because she hadn't planned to go to church that Sunday. She felt guilty because she wasn't going to church regularly. In fact, I think she struggled with it a lot. She had a hard time forgiving herself, even though the accident didn't involve anything she did or didn't do.

She was as good a mom as anyone could ever want. Years later, she was being interviewed by someone who was doing a newspaper story about the accident. There have been lots of media stories about it over the years. One of the most common questions journalists would ask about was how a person goes on with their life. You've seen those stories about how people turn tragedy into victory.

The interviewer asked her how she was able to put her guilt behind her. She didn't answer. She didn't look at the interviewer. The question was asked again. All my mom could say was, "I don't know." Then she got real quiet again.

Mom was in such pain about this happening to her child. She struggled with the fact that from time to time she couldn't make herself walk into the same room as me after my arms were amputated. But I don't remember it that way. What I remember is that she was there day and night. She was there all the time. But seeing her child in such agony was double torture for her.

I kept the job at the factory my whole five years of engineering school. After classes, I would go to work late in the afternoon. I would also work on Saturday mornings. That's the job that paid my way through college. The tedious work of doing drawings and learning to use the drawing instruments actually helped me in my engineering classes. The job tied in perfectly with what I planned to do with my life.

But let's get back to Sam for a minute. After I graduated from college and didn't work at the factory anymore, I lost touch with him. The next time I saw him was years later at my dad's funeral. I was asked to speak. Sam's son brought him to the graveside service in Weatherford. After all those years, he still had that hard shell. Looking at him was like looking at a brick wall. That's what he reminded me of, an arrogant brick wall that just seemed to dare you to step up to it, to try and get through it.

But seeing him that day, I realized that if I focused on him, I would go right back to resenting him. If I focused on Sam, the bitterness would again take root in my heart. It wouldn't hurt Sam. How could it? But it would destroy me. I had forgiven him. If I dwelt on his attitude or his lack of repentance, I would have been inviting the seed of bitterness to take root. So I prayed that I would focus on God and not on Sam.

Something I've found over the years is that forgiving a person once, doesn't mean it's all over. Old offenses can resurface many times in our lives. I've learned you have to forgive again and again, every time the offense resurfaces. I choose to forgive Sam.

Chapter 9

COLLEGE

Randy

There was an excitement about having my two mechanical arms. I was so glad to be able to do simple things again. When I got home from California, the first thing I wanted to do was get an attachment for my steering wheel so I could drive. My dad taught me to love cars from an early age and driving them is one of my favorite activities.

Being able to drive would give me mobility and freedom. I wanted to learn as quickly as I could. Some other things I was learning involved how to manipulate belts, zippers, and buttons. The more small tasks I could master with my hooks, the more freedom I could experience.

I had a deep sense of anticipation about starting college in the fall of 1967. I had always made good grades in high school. Because I had been ahead in earning credits, the accident in the spring of 1966 didn't keep me from graduating. Therefore, I was able to apply to attend the University of Texas at Arlington, which was in the center of the Dallas-Fort Worth metroplex. I was going to major in engineering.

UTA was close enough that I could live at home, work part-time at the factory, and attend college. That was really exciting. But it was also really intimidating. I was naturally shy and now I was starting college with two prosthetic arms.

I looked forward to college and making new friends. Most of my friends had moved on after high school. Vietnam was going on and some had gone into the military. Others had gone off to college. Even though I was excited about making new friends, it was scary. Nothing about the accident or my recovery made me any less shy.

This was long before the days when you registered for classes online. There wasn't an online on which to register. I had to go to the campus and stand in long lines with all the other students. Then we would pick up a schedule of all the class times and who was teaching what. After I had worked out my schedule, I went from table to table to register for classes. While standing in line on the first day of registration, I met some students who said, "Hey, we're having a party. We're a Christian club on campus and we want you to come."

Their building was actually right across the street from the registration lines. They said, "If you want to drop in, you can get out of the sun." I could see the building and the people were really friendly. That was a relief because I only knew two people who were going to UTA. That's out of a total enrollment of around twelve thousand students at that time.

The chances of seeing my friends were pretty slim. Also, UTA was a big commuter school, so people were coming and going all the time. It wasn't like a lot of colleges where most people lived on campus in the dorms.

After registration, I dropped in to see the people who had been so friendly. They were part of a group called the Baptist Student

Union or BSU. Nowadays that organization is called Baptist
Student Ministry or BSM. Some campuses call it Baptist Campus
Ministries. They are on hundreds, maybe thousands, of college
campuses all over North America. At UTA, the group still meets in
the same building. Only the carpet has changed.

The engineering school at UTA didn't have any casual seat-
ing areas. It was pretty stark and there was no place to relax.
Fortunately, I could walk over to the BSU and spend an hour
expanding my circle of friends. They really helped me work past
my shyness. Those people took me in and made me feel welcome.
I still thank God for that. I was a skinny, awkward young man with
two artificial arms. The people at the BSU were my age. I'm sure
they felt the same general awkwardness about life in college as I
did. Also, there wasn't so much awareness about dealing with and
accepting people with handicaps back then. But they cared about
me and welcomed me. Their building was a quiet place where I
could go for an hour or two between classes.

Having two artificial arms, everything took a lot longer. If other
people in the engineering department took twenty hours to do
their homework, it took me thirty-seven. I know because I kept a
log. I would start my homework in the evenings and finish around
eleven p.m. The writing took longer. So did the engineering drawings and moving weights and triangles. What my classmates could
do with the flick of a wrist took me multiple motions. I would also
have to set weights on the triangles to hold them in place while I
drew each line. It was a burdensome task just to finish a simple
homework assignment. And in engineering school, homework was
rarely simple.

To their credit and in spite of my disability, the professors were
very cautious to treat me the same as everyone else. I didn't find out
until after I graduated that some of the professors were taking my

drawings into other drafting classes and using them as an example of excellent work. The professor would say, "If a person who's been through an accident like that can do this quality of work, making all A's and B's, you guys ought to all be making straight A's."

My first semester, I tried taking seventeen hours of classes, but it was just too overwhelming. After that, I decided it didn't matter if it took me a semester longer to graduate. I could turn a four and a half year program into five years and make the pace more reasonable.

I always looked forward to lunchtime. On Mondays, Wednesdays, and Fridays the BSU had a brief program and then homemade sandwiches. Volunteers made the sandwiches and sold them for thirty-five cents. The price included chips and an iced tea. The money they raised went to fund summer mission trips. It cost a dollar and fifty cents to eat in the UTA cafeteria, so thirty-five cents at the BSU was a good deal.

Those were life-changing times for me. It was the beginning of what people called the Jesus Movement and there was a real excitement about the Lord. At that time, there was a nationwide revival and growing interest in spiritual things. People were questioning authority and that included the organized church.

There was also a lot of "God is dead" talk. Out of that came a burst of interest in God that put Jesus on the cover of *Time* magazine several times that decade. Christianity quit being so cut and dried. People weren't afraid to ask lots of questions, and eventually those questions led them back to God. Whether they accepted Him or rejected Him was up to them. But the questions at least took them to the right place.

Innovative Christian musicians were releasing exciting new songs that appealed to kids. There were love songs and ballads, even rock songs that talked about God. That was all new and the organized church wasn't sure how to handle it. I remember Billy Graham came to Dallas/Fort Worth to speak at Dallas Cowboys Stadium in Irving. That stadium was brand new at the time. We invited him to come to UTA and his organization said, "He will come as long as it's a unified invitation by all the Christian groups on campus."

All the Christian groups except one wanted him to speak on campus. It was an eye-opening experience how just a few contentious people with their own agenda can spoil some amazing things God wants to do. Can you imagine the impact it would have had if Billy Graham had spoken at UTA?

In spite of that, the word of God was being spread in a mighty way on the UTA campus. Our BSU director, Dan Bowling, organized a singing group of one hundred students called the Up Singers. During breaks between semesters, the organization would rent a school bus and go on tour. We sang all around the area. We also traveled down to Kingsville and Brownsville in South Texas. The drive took about twelve hours by bus each way.

While there, we sang in churches and schools along the Mexican border, as well as repairing widows' homes and doing other service projects. The next year there was a mission trip to Mexico. They wanted me to go. My concern was how I would do in group bathrooms and taking off and putting on my arms, as well as getting dressed. But they promised to help me with my arms and getting my coat on and off, that kind of thing. Those were real bonding times.

Going on that mission trip to Mexico also whetted my appetite for travel. That's something I hadn't ever really done before, except going to California to get my arms. The next year the Up Singers did another tour to the Rio Grande Valley of South Texas during spring break. My life became more and more centered around getting to do mission projects. God was bringing me out of my shell.

A lot of people who get involved in extra-curricular activities in college find that the "extra" becomes the main focus and they end up failing classes and having to drop out. I didn't want that to happen to me. I asked the Lord to help me. I said, "God, I want to be with my Christian friends. I want to travel with them. But I also need to take care of my studies. Help me to study and keep my grades up."

My motivation was to be with my Christian friends and serve the Lord. But I also knew I had an obligation to maintain my grades. One thing I realized was I'd have to not waste time daydreaming and just sitting around. When a person can get on a schedule and make efficient use of time, it's amazing how much he can accomplish.

You may have seen books on how to improve your study habits. Those were around back in the 1960s, too, and I read them. I also experimented with different techniques like scheduling my time. That helped me to get two hours of study into one hour on the clock.

Here's how scheduling works: I would write down everything I had to do. Then I would choose the hardest, most unpleasant task and start with it. I would book that task as taking fifty-five minutes. I forced my mind to focus intensely for power –learning the material. Then, I'd give myself a five minute break as a reward.

I'd then come back and hit the books again for another fifty-five minutes followed by another five minute reward. When I tackled the most difficult tasks first, that meant my day was getting easier and easier, not harder and harder. It also meant I had something to look forward to, not things still looming that I would dread.

Doing that made me very efficient. One mistake people often make is they put off the most difficult task for last because they don't want to do it. But that means you are tackling the most difficult task when you're the most tired. Doing it the other way around really helped me.

For me, that was huge. If I was efficient doing the things I needed to do, it made time for the things I wanted to do. That brought joy to my life. One of those things I wanted to do was called Friday Night Missions. Our BSU group partnered with a church in a high-poverty area, and we went there every Friday night.

We would spend time with neighborhood children. Being a low-income area, a lot of them came from single-parent families. Others came from really dysfunctional situations. We would go over and spend time with them. It was like a one-night Vacation Bible School that lasted all year long. I started going and the kids got used to my mechanical arms really quickly.

Friday Night Missions was a high point of my week. We would gather kids from all over the neighborhood at a small church. We would play games outside until darkness fell. Then we took them inside for Bible stories, singing, crafts, and times of getting to know them one-on-one. One night the group grew to about fifty kids and they were really rowdy.

The scheduled speaker didn't show up. Some of the BSU college students started asking who knew how to tell a Bible story. At the beginning of the year I had started reading the Bible through from cover to cover. I was to the third chapter of Daniel. That's the story of Shadrach, Meshach, and Abednego in the fiery furnace.

That story was on my mind, so I agreed to tell it to these fifty rambunctious kids. But first, I had to get their attention. I showed them how my arms worked and told them as dramatically as I could about my arms and also about some other people who had been through a fire. That night I learned how to tell a Bible story by just getting in there and doing it. I'd have to say that night was another turning point in my life.

I fell in love with speaking to those kids. As I told the story, I would watch their faces and see if they were getting it or not. It was easy to tell they were hanging on my every word. Watching their faces, I saw I was having a real impact. Also, I was telling them something of eternal consequence. God loved them and would see them through any tragedy.

Further, God can turn what Satan and the world meant for evil into good. Just look at me and what was happening at that moment. The kids really responded. In fact, several of them gave their hearts to Jesus that night. For the first time it was vividly demonstrated to me how God could use me to bring people to Him.

I mentioned earlier that two of my high school friends were also attending UTA. One of them nominated me to be the head of missions for the BSU. That was my sophomore year of college. I said I didn't think I could do it, but several people assured me it would only be for one semester. I thought, "I can try anything for one semester."

That was a really dynamic experience. We got to where we didn't just go out and do missions and then go our separate ways. We went to supper afterwards. We began to build a sense of community, doing things as a group. We would come back together, all the teams that had been in different neighborhoods, and meet at a local restaurant.

During that time, we would share our experiences, talk about what Jesus Christ had done and was doing in our lives, and have a laugh about funny things that happened. The social element really added to the ministry element. I learned people need and want to have fun together and that it, ultimately, builds a bond of unity.

My position as director of missions ended up lasting for two years. When I took the position, we had about five students regularly coming to our Friday night outreach. We grew that number to sixty. We kept hearing about other neighborhoods that wanted people to come and do some activities with their children.

We ended up sending groups of college students to five different neighborhoods each week. It didn't just help those children or the college students who went. It also helped me learn about organization and leading people. There were also a lot of strategic elements, such as making and executing a plan. Those are really important life skills. It's one thing to organize your own life. It's something else to organize and lead a group of other people. I had never done anything like that before. It was a really good experience.

My professional aspiration at that point was to be an engineer and invent new things. I wanted to work on large engineering projects designing machines. I was really interested in motion, machines, and physics. I also had some desire to develop electric-powered artificial arms. However, nobody was funding that type of work back then.

My senior engineering project was an electric elbow. That's what I needed most, so that's what I designed. By today's standards, it was really primitive. But it would have worked. Unfortunately, I didn't have the funds to actually build it. It would have been quite expensive. However, every engineer who looked at it told me, "This will definitely work."

While I was very focused on engineering and making good grades, you might say the gravitational center of my life began to change. I loved being with people and serving God. I was reading my Bible and my interest in spiritual concepts was growing.

Occasionally friends would change their focus from history or math to serving the needs of the world through Christian ministry. The thought crossed my mind. But then I saw myself in my mental mirror: very shy, skinny kid, probably the skinniest kid in the whole university, and with two artificial arms. Was there any way God could really use me?

I talked to some people I trusted and asked, "What if God is calling me to full-time ministry?" They were all pretty cool to the idea. The response was a sort of half-hearted, "Well, you know..." My own self-image didn't help things. I was stuck in the past. Shy, passive, lacking self-confidence.

About that time the BSU director, Dan Bowling, left to finish his PhD. Dan was a mentor who really understood the needs of college students. He was an encourager and a motivator. He was also a great organizer, putting together the Up Singers and all those mission trips. Dan was also really insightful. He could see the areas in your life where you really needed a push.

Through his mentoring I began leading people to Christ. Not just underprivileged kids, but intellectually driven college students and business professionals, as well. I enjoyed telling people about Jesus even more than I enjoyed engineering. Most of the people I knew in engineering were really lonesome. They had their work, but no joy in their lives. I had the intellectual challenge of engineering but I also had friends, joy, music, fun, and Jesus. I also had an emerging self-confidence.

However, the Bible teaches that there is a spiritual war going on every day. I can testify that it's true. Satan knew I was making a difference in people's lives for Christ. He was determined to get me derailed. And he tried to use some very "religious" people to do it.

Lots of people were interested in spiritual things. It was common during that period to talk about different belief systems and religious experiences. I ran into a group of people who were teaching that Jesus' real power was based on His discovery of a new way to pray.

They said His miracles were an answer to prayer because He used this technique. They taught Jesus wanted us to use this "special technique," too. As a young Christian, I was vulnerable to their teachings because it all sounded pretty good.

They supported their points with examples from the book of John in the New Testament. I began attending their classes. These sessions turned into self-hypnosis training and grew from that point to self-suggestion, mental programing, and then into some really bizarre stuff like séances.

This was all part of something called mind control. The people involved in it said it was the technique used in the Bible for spiritual healing, spiritual communication, imagination sensitizing, and other things such as extra-sensory perception, and a lot of things that border on the occult.

I carefully observed these people and noticed something very interesting about them. They kept talking about peace and God and more meaningful lives. But what I saw was they were all very suspicious of each other. Whereas I saw joy in the lives of the people in our Bible study groups and Friday Night Missions, I saw paranoia and an obsessive fear in the other group. However, I was fascinated with this group and what they were teaching. So they continued to lure me in.

Another thing I realized was that, as I got deeper into mind control, I began losing confidence in my God-given abilities. I saw my joy slipping away. I also became preoccupied with a fear of the unknown. I saw myself beginning to pull away from my relationship with Christ.

I never intended for mind control to take me away from Jesus. I was looking for something that would help me be a better Christian. That wasn't what these people were offering. They were taking me down a completely different path.

One day in our weekly BSU council meetings, I began to share what I had experienced in this other group. Our new director, Rollin DeLap, looked me straight in the eyes and said, "Randy, Jesus has everything you need." That's all he said. That's all he needed to say. The statement burned into my mind. I began to think, "Who and what am I putting my trust in, Jesus or my ability to channel certain techniques?" I realized that all this pseudo-occult stuff was sabotaging my relationship with Jesus Christ.

The people in the BSU cared enough about me to try and set me straight. They emphasized the importance of scripture memorization, staying focused on God's Word, prayer, serving others, and giving. I began to spend more time memorizing scripture. The security of being God's child, and the power of the Holy Spirit, began to return to my life.

As I began to memorize Bible verses, I found my joy coming back. I abandoned the other group and all their techniques and self-hypnosis. All their teachings about spiritual power were based in what people did, not what God did through people. Later it dawned on me I was experimenting with a cult group. At the time I never even realized it. That's how deceptive these kinds of groups can be.

In fact, science has disproven most of this group's theories about how the brain works, but that hasn't slowed them down. Where it began to get weird was when they started talking about spiritual guides visiting you. Once my eyes were opened, I realized these were nothing more than demonic presences. I got away from it as quick as I could.

As the joy returned and the scripture memorization increased, I started on a scripture memory system of sixty verses. I began to tell more people around the UTA campus about Jesus. One day I was talking to this guy who was working on his master's degree in psychology. I had the chance to share Jesus with him and actually led him to the Lord.

People even told me they thought I might have the gift of evangelism. If that was true, I wanted to use that gift at every opportunity to share Jesus. I didn't just *want* to talk about Jesus Christ; I *enjoyed* talking about Him. One year I was able to lead fifty-three people to the Lord.

What does that mean? It means helping people transfer their hope and trust from their own competency, good works, and performance to trusting in the life, teachings, and power of Jesus. Further, Christians believe that all people have a capacity to know God, but have closed off their access to Him through disobedience. Christians call this sin. This sin builds a barrier between people and God. That's the bad news.

The good news is that God Himself reached out to all people through the person of His son, Jesus Christ. Jesus' perfect life and sacrificial death on the cross provided satisfaction for the penalty of sin. God made a bridge between Himself and us in the person of Jesus. Simply put, Jesus showed us the way, taught us God's values, and paid the penalty for all of our disobedience. We then have the opportunity to respond by believing in Him and asking Him to forgive our sin and change our lives through His Spirit and truth. To lead someone to the Lord is simply answering their questions with what the Bible teaches. Then you invite them to transfer their trust from themselves to Jesus, accepting His offer of eternal life.

Chapter 10

ROAD TRIP

Randy

During the fall of 1969 we got word there was going to be a huge youth conference in Atlanta, Georgia, called Mission '70. It was scheduled for the week between Christmas and New Years and would provide education and inspiration on hundreds of ministry opportunities in the United States and around the world. We heard up to five thousand college students would attend.

It would also include a lot of community projects in the inner-city Atlanta area, like what we had been doing in the poor areas of Arlington. Some guys from the BSU wanted to go. They didn't have to ask me twice. I was beginning to seriously consider missions for my own life, so it was a golden opportunity.

We borrowed a church van and five of us drove across country to the event. We all became lifetime friends. Even though I was still living at home, I didn't have any extra money. I did get some remuneration from Workman's Compensation for losing both arms. It was thirty-five dollars a week for seven years. I was also working two hours a day at American Manufacturing and four hours each Saturday. But seeing my dad at work those two hours each weekday made me even more convinced maybe engineering wasn't for me.

When I looked at him, he seemed so lonely. He was a genius, but very lonely.

The alcohol consumption was also becoming more and more of a problem. My sister Nancy had seen how the church had reached out to our family after the accident. It really helped her and my brother Rex to get plugged into church regularly. However, my dad just checked out. That loneliness and despair, the rejection of the one thing that could bring real joy – a relationship with Jesus – could be contrasted with what I saw at Mission '70. Those were exciting days of incredibly gifted speakers, mission projects, and seeing what could be accomplished by people unified under Jesus Christ. I continued to ask, "God, could you really be calling me into full-time service?"

I also remember saying, "God, I don't think I could do anything for you. I know I can do engineering. I'm good at that. But I'm not a public speaker, even though, yes, I can talk to little kids on Friday nights. I know I can learn about the Bible and work to be a soul winner, but..." I just didn't know.

When the BSU director, Dan Bowling, left to finish his PhD, he was followed by Rollin Delap. Rollin was the fellow I referred to earlier who shared with me the importance of memorizing scripture and being involved in discipleship. Rollin was the person God used to steer me away from the whole mind control cult. As a student, he left civil engineering to transfer to an evangelical Christian college and begin to disciple young people.

I was already on the BSU executive council and we were planning and budgeting for the year. Rollin also invited each of us to have a private thirty-minute life coaching session each week with him. He would challenge us, "You could grow faster as a believer if you were interested in and would become committed to memorizing scripture."

A lot of times when people hear others talk about scripture memorization, they kind of wince. However, I think of scripture as being your spiritual alphabet. The alphabet isn't an end to itself, but rather a way to make words and meaning. Knowing scripture and being able to recall it helps us to make meaning out of life.

Rollin Delap challenged me to memorize sixty scripture verses. In fact, he said, "You can't really be a functional Christian leader without these sixty verses. So I memorized two a week. A lot of the fear and intimidation I had been feeling started to fall by the wayside. God gave me more boldness as I memorized more scripture. It is a way to learn God's truth. Rollin said, "Spend time with God and let Him direct you."

Memorizing those sixty verses didn't happen overnight. It took a year to learn them all. I also had to keep up with my studies in engineering, working in neighborhood ministry, and other projects. We also had mission trips and opportunities to lead people to Jesus Christ.

Something else happened about that time. The BSU asked me to change from the missions committee to chairing the work with international students and leading evangelism training. My last year at college, I was also program chairman for the three days each week when people were invited to BSU for lunch and to listen to a guest speaker. It was hectic and fabulous.

When it came to international students, I loved learning about world religions so I could interact with those from other faiths in a meaningful way. One way the BSU did that was by inviting foreign students to a spring retreat. We had speakers at these retreats who were there to explain Christianity. These were people like Bill Hendricks who was one of the top Christian evangelists and thinkers in the country at that time.

I discovered that asking international students about their country and what life was like for them was a good way to build a relationship. They travel all the way to the United States and very few people notice them. They are pretty much alone for four, five, or six years doing their studies. Because we expressed an interest in them, several of the internationals invited us over to their apartments and cooked meals for us.

One night I was talking to a Hindu who was a straight A engineering student. There was a four-foot-tall water color picture of a Hindu god on his living room wall. I asked him what his god was like. He said that his god was a great warrior who got his head cut off and was given the head of an elephant and extra arms. My Hindu friend believed in this elephant god and prayed to it. The main thing he could tell me about this god was that because he had the head of an elephant, he had a great memory and never forgot anything. The god is called Ganesha and he is the god of success in Hinduism.

I wanted a way to share with people the difference between myths and Biblical truth. I wanted to convey the difference between these sort of mythical stories and the stories in the Bible. When people investigate the claims in the Bible, they find there are thousands of years of prophecies that came true. They can also see this wasn't just something somebody claimed, but that these events in the Bible were witnessed by hundreds or thousands of people.

As I approached graduation, I was praying, asking God if I should continue to pursue engineering or take a year off to attend a Bible college. There was also a new program called Student to Student started by the BSU. People were asking me if I was going to apply. They thought it would be a good fit for me. It was an opportunity to serve Christ and reach people for Him. Today it is called the Campus Evangelism Coordinator. The job description was to take all that I learned as a student, move to another campus, and be a peer who could rally other students to witness and share Christ.

The goal was to start new Bible studies on university campuses around the state. We would focus on basic questions about who God is, who Jesus is, and so forth. At the same time, American Manufacturing was planning on me graduating and becoming one of their full-time engineers. My dad was also planning on that. I felt really torn about what to do.

My plan was to use my talents as an engineer as a platform to help the world and talk to other engineers about Christ. That would also allow me to support myself and a family one day. But as I continued to pray about it, I realized that for me, the right direction, the direction God was calling me in, was full-time ministry.

Of course, for Christians the secret isn't being a full-time minister. Ministers are just people. God calls all of us to set aside our agenda and follow His will, whatever it is. Once I made that choice to surrender to God's will, it created a real peace of mind. My favorite Bible verse at the time was Matthew 6:33, which says to seek first the Kingdom of God and His righteousness ahead of everything else. Once I made the decision to do that, the other areas of life began to fall into place.

Let me add that when we are seeking God's will, the emphasis of our prayers shouldn't be on what we are going to do for a living, but rather on being more like Jesus. We need to become the people God wants us to be, and then the occupational issues fall into place. All Christians are called to be ministers and serve the Lord, regardless of what their career might be.

Let me add that If your life outlook is that you want to rule, your job opportunities are pretty limited. If you are willing to serve, the world is full of opportunities. Our focus through prayer and Bible study is to be more like Christ. The goal is to raise up qualified, committed Christian laborers who are teachers or insurance salesmen, or whatever. But for me, the call was to full-time ministry. So I did apply for the Student to Student program. To my shock, they wanted me.

My first assignment was Southwest Texas State University, which is now Texas State University, in San Marcos. It was a beautiful place. Being a teachers college, it seemed like all the pretty girls from South Texas who were going to be educators were going there. I might add I moved from UTA, a campus with five guys to every girl, to Texas State, which had five girls for every guy. The scenery improved dramatically. But we had a no dating policy for those on staff of the BSU. I was a kid in a candy store, but it wasn't meant to be.

Student to Student started in 1972. We almost immediately doubled the number of people participating in BSU across the state of Texas. At Southwest Texas State, I recruited thirty-five students, mostly freshmen, to try leading outreach Bible studies with their friends. The studies were organized to cover a new topic each week for ten weeks. They answered people's questions about God, Jesus, the church, and so forth. They were only intended to last ten weeks. Interest and involvement was so high, twenty-one of them lasted the entire school year. We also gave Good News New Testament Bibles to thousands of college students.

My time at Southwest Texas State went so well the BSU state organization asked me to begin traveling around Texas as a field trainer. I would travel on Sunday afternoon, be at a campus on Monday, and take people out witnessing. I would travel to big schools like Texas Tech for a week and smaller schools like community colleges for three days.

It meant a lot of driving. For those who don't know, Texas is a huge state. It is larger than the entire country of France. Traveling from El Paso in West Texas to Beaumont in southeast Texas takes almost twelve hours by car. But I was excited to do it. I moved across the state teaching Christian college students how to share their faith. At the same time, I got to know and share with many international students. I helped them see the truth about Christ, as well as the difference He made in my life.

I realized during this time that there is a vast difference between being a believer and really letting God get a hold on my life. My prayers went from, "God, I love you, but I don't think I could serve you in a full-time way," to "God, I want to serve you with everything that's in me."

At that point, I began to really want to go to seminary. I knew I could always go back to engineering, but this might be my last chance to study theology. Also, Rollin said if I was ever going to serve, I needed formal training. That would be my credibility with people who might hire me to work in ministry.

At the same time, the BSU wanted me to delay going to seminary to continue working with Student to Student. I'm glad I did. Not only did it allow me to share Christ; it also led me to Lubbock and Texas Tech University. It was there I would meet the woman who would become my wife.

RANDY WORKED FOR FIFTY CENTS AN HOUR TO BUY SOME
WHEELS, INCLUDING A CAR AND MOTOR SCOOTER.

RANDY AND LITTLE BROTHER REX ENJOYING PLAYTIME.

RANDY WITH HIS FATHER, NORRIS, MOTHER, VIRGINIA, BROTHER, REX, SISTER, NANCY. THIS PICTURE WAS TAKEN LESS THAN A YEAR BEFORE THE ACCIDENT.

PASTOR JARVIS PHILPOT, FORTY-SEVEN YEARS AFTER
THE ACCIDENT, CONTINUES TO BE A GREAT INFLUENCE
ON RANDY'S LIFE. IN THE BACKGROUND IS A PICTURE OF
PASTOR PHILPOT ABOUT THE TIME OF THE ACCIDENT.

RANDY'S MOM
STOOD BY HIM,
PROVIDING
CEASELESS
ENCOURAGEMENT
THROUGH THIRTY-
EIGHT SURGERIES.

RANDY AND MARY ANN AT THEIR WEDDING, JUNE 27, 1975.

MARY ANN'S PARENTS, RAY
AND MARIE MILLIKEN, HELPED
START SOUTHCREST BAPTIST
CHURCH IN LUBBOCK, TEXAS.

MARY ANN AND BROTHER, MIKE MILLIKEN. WHILE
AT WORK, HE WAS SHOT SIX TIMES BY ROBBERS.

HENRY BLACKABY,
AUTHOR OF
EXPERIENCING GOD,
CONTINUES TO BE
A MAJOR FORCE IN
THE LIVES OF RANDY
AND MARY ANN.

RANDY AND MARY ANN WITH CHILDREN JOHN, AGE FIVE,
AND AMY, ALMOST FOUR, IN 1989. DURING THAT PERIOD,
THEY WERE MOVING FROM VANCOUVER TO TORONTO.

RANDY ADDRESSED
NEARLY TEN THOUSAND
PEOPLE AT MISSION 90 IN
FORT WORTH, TEXAS.

RANDY AND MARY ANN WITH JOHN, AGE
SEVENTEEN, AND AMY, AGE FIFTEEN, IN 2001.

MARY ANN ALWAYS
WANTED TO LIVE IN
A PLACE WITH REAL
WINTERS. CANADA
PROVIDED THAT
OPPORTUNITY.

RANDY AND MARY ANN WITH A GROUP OF
TORONTO UNIVERSITY STUDENTS.

RANDY AND MARY ANN
CLIMBING THE GREAT
WALL OF CHINA.

RANDY IN FRONT OF A COLLAPSED SCHOOL IN WENCHUAN, CHINA. WHEN THE 2008 EARTHQUAKE HIT, THOUSANDS DIED. THE RUBBLE OF THE SCHOOL BECAME A MEMORIAL.

RANDY SPEAKING IN THE EARTHQUAKE AREA. HIS MESSAGE, NEVER GIVE UP, IS A CHALLENGE TO REMAIN HOPEFUL EVEN IF THE WORLD AROUND YOU COLLAPSES.

RANDY WITH KATE AND HER HUSBAND
CHARLES AT THEIR WEDDING. RANDY'S
MINISTRY PROVIDED ARTIFICIAL LEGS FOR
KATE AFTER THE EARTHQUAKE IN 2008.

RANDY WITH CHINESE
MINISTRY PARTNER AND
FRIEND, MILLER ZHUANG.

RANDY AND MARY ANN'S SON, JOHN, WITH HIS
WIFE, CHELSEA, AND THEIR CHILDREN, AUSTIN
AND GRACYN, IN 2013. THE LEGACY OF HOPE
CONTINUES WITH A NEW GENERATION.

Chapter 11

UNIQUE AND DIFFERENT

Mary Ann

My mother, Marie Milliken, was a nurse. She grew up on a cotton farm in West Texas. She said there were three choices for women in her day. You could be a farmer's wife, a school teacher, or a nurse. She went to nursing school. One of my uncles spoke for a lot of people when he said, "If there had been the money to send her to medical school, she would have been a great doctor. She had the brains for it."

She moved from a farm near the little town of Denver City, Texas, to Lubbock, about an hour and a half away, to attend nursing school. At that time, Lubbock had a population of about seventy-one thousand. After nursing school, she became a night shift supervisor at Highland Hospital, working from 11 p.m. to 7 a.m. in the emergency room. That was back in the days when doctors were at home and they were called in to the hospital if there was an emergency. That meant the nursing staff was responsible for getting the patient stabilized until the doctor could get there. Of course, it was a huge responsibility. So at a time when men were in charge of most things, my mother was in charge of a lot of people.

When I came along, I remember being told, "You don't have to be limited in your choices. You can be anything you want to be." I was born in 1952 and that's not the kind of things most little girls were being told at that time. The women's liberation movement was still a decade or two away. Mother would say, "You're smart, you like science, you like math. You can do anything."

My father would say, "If you give it your best, that's fine. You don't have to make straight A's, but you do have to try hard and do your best."

Both my parents were committed Christians. They cared for each other. They were honest. They cared about others. They didn't just talk about helping people; they helped them. They lived by the Ten Commandments and were extremely kind and compassionate. In fact, being compassionate was something our family emphasized. Once a month we would go visit my grandparents back on the farm. My Uncle Charlie, my mom's youngest brother, had Down's syndrome. Charlie had the mental function of about a four- or five-year-old. We were taught to be kind to Charlie.

By the time all the grandkids were seven or eight, we realized we had more mental capacity than Charlie did, even though he was much older. But if anybody made fun of Charlie or teased him, that was a quick way to get a spanking. You just didn't do that. Charlie was a human being and all human beings were to be treated with dignity.

And it wasn't just about being thoughtful to your family. You acted respectful and demonstrated kindness to everyone. My mom and dad both worked outside the home, and sometimes they would hire housekeepers of a variety of races. It didn't matter the color of their skin – white, African-American, Hispanic – these ladies were adults and I was to treat them as such. One time I said something to one of the ladies in the wrong tone. I was quickly taken to another room and reminded, "This lady is your elder. All people are created equal and you will not speak to another human being, regardless of race or circumstance, in that tone. Do you understand?"

I understood.

That was a time when it was common to hear white people refer to those of other races using very derogatory terms, even in public. However, my parents said their rule for our family was that you just didn't talk about other people using derogatory terms or a disrespectful manner. This was back in the 1950s and early 60s, so not everybody, even other Christians, felt that way. But our family emphasized being accepting and kind.

As a little girl I remember getting together with friends. There would be conversations about who each of us were going to some-day marry. I remember my mother had two conditions regarding who I married. The first was he needed to be a hard worker who could make a good living for his family. The second was that he needed to be a committed Christian.

I was always telling my mom, "I want to be a doctor, so it doesn't matter what my husband does." She would say, "That's fine. But if you decide you want to stay home and raise your kids, you need a hard worker who can make a good living for you."

My father, Ray, worked at the Texas Employment Commission. There were people who would come in, day after day, and give all these sad stories about why they never could find a job. He really believed in hard work without making excuses. Hearing all these stories from people trying to get out of work only reinforced that feeling.

While my mother was working as the head of the emergency room she got an ulcer and had to stay home for a while. When she was better, she got a job at the health department as a visiting nurse. She would walk into all kinds of homes and all kinds of situations with all kinds of people. While she had compassion for everyone, it still reminded her of the importance of hard work.

During my junior year of high school, which was in 1969, my mother was approached by a businessman who said he wanted to open the first home healthcare agency in Lubbock. He also wanted her to run it. Home health agencies were brand new back then. Professional nurses would go into people's residences to provide the care they needed instead of them being put into a nursing home. Again, she was walking into all kinds of situations and dealing with all kinds of people.

She accepted the offer and built a business starting with three people in Lubbock. Within a few years there were over five hundred employees. She opened offices in nine different cities from Dumas in the Texas Panhandle to Kerrville in the Texas Hill Country. I remember once in 1971 she came home from an out-of-town meeting. At that meeting she heard about another new service called Meals on Wheels. It provided free lunch to home-bound people, along with someone to check on them Monday through Friday of every week.

On her first day back from the meeting, she walked into the home health agency. There were four nurses sitting there. She said, "Our people need this. You ladies are all registered nurses and highly capable. Between the four of you, decide which one is going to resign from West Texas Home Health to start Meals on Wheels." She promised that whoever made the choice to start Meals on Wheels would still have the same paycheck.

"Just decide which one of you wants to do it," she said. I was working part-time at the home health agency. I was there when it happened. A few days later, Mary Williams, one of the four nurses, said she had been praying about it. She believed it was what God wanted her to do. That's how Meals on Wheels started in Lubbock, Texas.

I was seventeen at the time. You can see that my entire life I was surrounded by the idea that you help others. My mom's commitment to helping people wasn't just words. It was action. For her, that included traveling to the state capitol in Austin, Texas, and to Washington, D.C., to help craft legislation that would govern how other home health agencies would operate on both the state and national level.

When my mom died in 2004, I got a call from a man in Austin who said, "Your mother was one of the two founding women of home health agencies in the entire nation. Your mother was an incredible lady." She started on a humble farm, got a three-year nursing degree, and grew to lead hundreds of people and impact health and wellness across the entire country.

Not only was I affected by my mom; I was also affected by what I read. At age twelve, I read a book called *The Family Nobody Wanted* by Helen Doss. The author's husband was a Methodist minister and they adopted all these orphans nobody wanted. The children represented thirty-five different nationalities. Reading that true story had a profound effect on how I thought about people who were in need, and my attitudes about bringing them into my family.

So at the age of twelve, I walked into the kitchen and announced to my mom, "I don't care if I ever give birth to children. I just want to adopt." My thinking on adoption, and I think this came from reading *The Family Nobody Wanted*, is that the color of someone's skin is like the wrapping paper on a Christmas present. Nobody sits there and just looks at the paper all day. You look past the paper and see what's inside. It's what's inside that counts. That theme has run throughout my life.

My dad and his family also influenced my thinking on how you treat people. Dad was the oldest of seven. One of his sisters was two years younger than him. She was on the island of Oahu in Hawaii the day Pearl Harbor was bombed by the Japanese. She and her husband couldn't have children so they adopted a full-blooded Hawaiian girl. Her name is Claudia.

Therefore, growing up I had an adopted Hawaiian cousin. They started out living in Hawaii, but later moved to Houston. We didn't see them very often, but when we did, it was understood that this child was as much a part of the family as if she had been born to them.

My grandparents also modeled treating everyone with respect. There was a sense of inclusion on both sides of the family; there was Uncle Charlie who had a handicap and Claudia who was adopted. Everyone was treated the same. If you were adopted into our family, you belonged.

So that deeply affected my thoughts on whom I would marry one day. I remember one time when I was a girl, my parents took me on a two-week camping vacation across the southern U.S. to see the giant redwoods in California. I was able to invite a friend and chose to invite a girl named Vickie. There was a camper on the back of the family pickup and Vickie and I rode in the camper. My parents couldn't hear us, so we talked about all the things girls talk about: What we wanted to do when we grew up, what kind of a person we wanted to marry, you know.

I told Vickie, "I want someone who is a committed Christian. But I feel really impressed I'm going to marry someone unique and different." I told her this man would be in the ministry, but not a pastor, because I didn't feel led to be a pastor's wife." When we started talking about having children, I told her I wanted to adopt.

111

"Oh, I could never do that!" Vickie said. I asked why, adding a baby was a baby and they all need love. She said she could never love a child that wasn't born to her. I was totally surprised. I felt, and still feel, that every child needs love. If you can adopt a child and give him or her love, I think that is a very important thing.

As we talked more, Vickie revealed she never wanted to go anywhere. She was happy to stay right where she was in Lubbock. I wanted to travel, to live in different places, places with four distinct seasons; a place with real winter and lots of snow. My impression back then was it might be the West Coast or the Pacific Northwest. As an adolescent, I thought everyone probably had the same kinds of dreams and aspirations. Talking to Vickie during those two weeks convinced me that wasn't necessarily true.

At the age of thirteen I felt impressed to commit my life to a call of special service to the Lord. I didn't even really understand what that meant, but I felt a very clear impression it would involve travel. I never wanted to be the kind of person whose world view ended at the city limits sign.

When it came time to go to college, I became a pre-med major at Texas Tech. I began attending the Baptist Student Union meetings, got involved in Freshman Council, and Friday Night Missions. There were also leadership conferences in the fall and spring in Dallas or Waco. We also had annual trips to a large Christian camp at Glorieta, New Mexico, right outside of Santa Fe. I first attended Glorieta as a teenager for church youth camp. It was a very important place to me. It was exciting to be able to continue that tradition even as a college student. For me, a lot of very special times with the Lord and other people are associated with Glorieta.

Through the BSU I applied to be a summer missionary. I wanted to work at a Spanish-speaking church in Los Angeles. I had been around Spanish-speaking people since I was a child because my grandfather hired a lot of Latinos to work on his farm. I started taking Spanish lessons in seventh grade and continued right on through college.

One semester I participated in a study-abroad program, going to Mexico and taking classes in Spanish. During the time we were there, we stayed in the homes of Mexican nationals. We also got to tour the sights in Mexico City. I loved the culture and looked forward to getting to work in a Spanish-speaking church during summer missions.

Another interest of mine was sign language. We attended Southcrest Baptist, a church in Lubbock my parents helped to start. But one of the other churches in town, First Baptist, offered sign language lessons on Sunday nights. My friend Helen Nagle and I attended the classes. We really enjoyed learning sign language and I think I was pretty good at signing.

As part of the application process for summer missions, I had to travel to Dallas to interview. There were six of us girls who carpooled. The interviews were set up throughout the day and I had the last slot before lunch. The interview committee was made up of six or seven people. One of them was a guy named Randy Gallaway.

Randy was on the committee as a student representative from UTA. I was an extremely shy person – I still am – and all I can remember about the interview was the six or seven faces of the interview committee members staring at me. When my interview was over, everyone came out of the room and waited at the elevator. That was when I really noticed Randy.

The first thing that struck me was the hook on his left arm. His other hand looked like a real hand, but maybe with a glove over it. Then I realized it was an artificial hand. I thought that was interesting; certainly unique and different.

As it turned out, I was accepted by the committee and became a summer missionary to the Spanish-speaking community in Los Angeles, California. One of the churches I worked with was attended by a Spanish-speaking couple who had a deaf son. I ended up translating from Spanish to English to sign language and vice versa to help him communicate. It was a great experience.

Meanwhile, that was the same summer Randy went to spend a year at Southwest Texas State University at San Marcos, now Texas State University, leading Bible studies. Then he spent a semester traveling, leading Bible studies, and teaching college students how to share their faith. That was the fall of 1973.

Randy had a real gift for evangelism, was an excellent speaker, and had a powerful testimony. At one point there was a student conference with five thousand people attending. Randy was there to tell the story of his accident and how God had worked in his life. Randy also traveled to twenty-eight campuses across Texas. One of those was Texas Tech, where I attended. When he finished speaking, people would flock to talk to him. Let me tell you about Randy. He was one of the really important people in college ministry in the entire state. If he came to your campus, people talked about it for days.

I was very, very shy, so I didn't talk to him. However, I had been thinking I really needed to break out of my shell. One way I decided to do that was to go up and speak to one of the presenters who came to talk to us. I was determined to tell the person what a good job he did. I was hoping it would help me get over being so shy. There were ten people presenting in October of 1973 during an evangelism conference at Texas Tech. The person I decided to go up and talk to was Randy.

Chapter 12

LOVE AND DENNY'S

Randy

In the fall of 1973 I was traveling all over Texas working with people on how to share their faith. There was a huge evangelism thrust underway at Texas Tech University in Lubbock. They brought in some special speakers for a week of outreach. It was based out of the BSU.

Keep in mind that in those days in West Texas, almost everyone had some sort of church background. They had a grandma or a mom or dad who prayed for them. Divorce was still very rare and most families were still together. There also hadn't been the breakdown of trust in society that we see today. However, the Watergate Scandal was just starting to come into the public attention. People were also learning that the government had lied about a lot of the things done during the Vietnam War through the Pentagon Papers, which were leaked to the public.

In spite of that, or maybe because of it, people were generally willing to listen to you and talk about what they believed spiritually. We could go knock on doors and people would talk to us. Sometimes they would even invite us in. When I said, "I'm from such-and-such church," people respected the fact I had the courage of my convictions and appreciated I was willing to get out and share what I believed.

The attitude was, "Oh, you Christians are the nice people who built the nice churches and put on the Vacation Bible School my kids love attending." In spite of that, many Christians still needed the boldness to share what Jesus Christ had done for them. My job was to help them share their faith with others.

One of the downsides of doing campus ministry is that it was forbidden for me to date any of the students, even though we were all about the same age. I completely understood. I was on staff. They couldn't have someone abusing their position to get dates. But when I was approached about traveling around the state I said, "Okay, but since I won't be on staff at those schools. If I find someone I want to ask out, can I date them?"

I was told it would be handled on a case-by-case basis. I would have to clear it first with the BSU director on each campus. That's because he would be the best person to understand each situation. Mary Ann was super shy, even more shy than I was. But she prayed to have the courage to go up to a speaker and talk to the person after their presentation.

After I shared my testimony, she came up and asked if I would go with her to visit an atheist student she had met in one of her classes. I said yes and we set it up for a couple of nights later. The three of us went out for pizza and talked. The atheist shared his beliefs and we shared ours. After we dropped him off, Mary Ann and I talked for a while; two or three more hours, actually. That started our friendship.

To show you how phenomenal a time it was and how the Lord was moving, one night during that week, I was invited over to a dorm to pray for the people who lived there. We ended up talking to some of the guys standing in a doorway. I shared my testimony and extended an invitation. Six or seven of the guys had been listening in. They ended up praying to receive Jesus Christ as their Savior and Lord right then and there. The Lord was moving in an incredible way.

Later that week, I spoke to an auditorium full of students at the Lubbock Coliseum. The meeting was called Campus Evangelism Thrust. There were other speakers, as well. After it was over, everyone was standing around talking. A large group was going to Denny's. Mary Ann asked me if I wanted to ride with her. I excused myself and went over to find her BSU director. I asked him if it was alright to ask her out for a date.

I had a lot of apprehension. When I dated someone, it was usually just one or two dates and then she would marry someone else. I used to joke that if a girl was looking for a husband, all she had to do was go out with me. The next thing you knew, the man of her dreams would appear. But at the time, all I was thinking about was what a fantastic week it had been and that Mary Ann had invited me to go to Denny's with her.

I was really happy around Mary Ann. But there was also fear. The strain in my parents' marriage had finally reached a crisis point and they divorced. Unfortunately, divorce was becoming more and more common. I had several high school friends who had married and were already divorced. Society was really changing. There were very few role models in my life to show what a happy family looked like.

Nonetheless, her BSU director said it was fine to ask her out. I had a spark of interest and I wanted to find out if she did, too. With my two artificial arms, I was not the most desirable bachelor on the block.

Chapter 13

A FAITHFUL CHRISTIAN AND HARD WORKER

Mary Ann

It took all the courage I could muster to initiate a conversation with Randy near the beginning of the Campus Evangelism Thrust. When Randy spoke, it was on the importance of scripture memory. I had been talking to this guy named Jeff in my microbiology class who was an atheist. It occurred to me if there was anybody this guy would listen to, it was Randy.

When I approached Randy, he was willing to talk to Jeff. I also talked to Jeff and found he was willing to talk to Randy. I picked them both up at 5 o'clock to go eat pizza. That was on Wednesday night. We talked to Jeff for about two hours. After we dropped him off, Randy and I talked for another three hours. That was the start of our relationship.

On Friday night, the last night of the conference, we met at the Lubbock Coliseum. Afterward, a large group was going to Denny's and I asked Randy if he wanted to ride with me. Before he went with me though, he went over to talk to my BSU director. I couldn't hear what they were talking about and had no idea it involved me.

The conversation lasted about one minute. I figured they were thanking each other for a nice week.

I can't remember whether it was that night or later, but I eventually found out Randy's conversation with my BSU director was to get permission to ask me out. There was a rule BSU directors couldn't date students on the campuses where they work. When Randy was asked to travel, he said, "I'm going to twenty-eight different campuses and I won't be at any of them very long. If I find someone I would like to have a date with, can I ask her?"

When Randy came back over from talking to my BSU director, we went to Denny's with twelve other people. Randy was sitting at the end of the table and I was sitting on one side, closest to him. I thought we were all just friends, but Randy started flirting.

How do you know somebody's flirting if they don't have hands? As he was talking to me, he was kind of gently bumping my knee with his knee. Suddenly it occurred to me: he likes me. After dinner, I took him back to his car and we talked for another couple of hours. I had no idea it was a date. However, he asked my BSU director if he could go out with me, the BSU director said okay, and we ended up talking for several hours. It was our first date.

Afterward, I just had to tell someone about this incredible experience. I didn't feel like I could talk to anyone at Texas Tech, but I had to tell someone. I decided to tell my friend Alana Havens. She was going to college at Hardin-Simmons in Abilene, Texas. That's about three hours from Lubbock. I asked my parents if I could go down and see her for the weekend.

They said yes, so I called Alana and set it up. Keep in mind this was before the days of unlimited nationwide long distance, email, and Facebook. Long distance telephone calls were expensive, so it made a lot more sense to just go down there and see her.

On Friday I headed for Abilene and spent the night with Alana. Then, the next day, I drove three more hours to see Randy and his mother in Dallas/Fort Worth. My parents didn't know about that. I spent the night at a cousin's house in the area.

When I was in Fort Worth, Randy and I went to Jimmy Dips Chinese Restaurant. We talked about our relationship and decided to just see where the Lord would lead us. We knew a long-distance relationship would not be easy. Then, on Sunday, I stopped back by Alana's for lunch. I told her this might be the person I would marry, but asked her not to tell anyone.

I explained to her why I thought Randy might be the one. He was a committed Christian leader who worked in ministry with the BSU. He was also unique and different. He wasn't a pastor and didn't want to be a pastor. He fit all the things I had sensed would be in my future husband.

Though Randy and I liked each other, long-distance dating wasn't easy. It involved a lot of expensive phone calls, letter writing, and prearranged meetings. If I was traveling to see him, I stayed with a mutual friend named Barbara Burkett or with Randy's mother at her house. When Randy came to Lubbock, he would take me to Texas Tech football games. It was really exciting dating Randy. So many people on the Tech campus knew him and loved to listen to him speak. They would see him in Lubbock and ask me, "Is he speaking somewhere around here?"

I would tell them no and they'd ask, "Well, then why is he here?" Then I would tell them he was here to see me. It was like dating a movie star or a celebrity. There were about one hundred and twenty students in the BSU at that time and they all loved Randy.

In March of 1974, Randy came to Lubbock to be the speaker at a retreat. I volunteered to go out to the airport to pick him up. That gave us several hours alone to visit. I took him by to see a house my parents had just bought in Lubbock. They had moved into the house about eleven days earlier.

After that, we dated long distance until January 1975. During one of our conversations, Randy insisted I ask my parents if they were okay with me marrying someone without arms. I told him they were fine with it. They always told me they wanted my future husband to be a hard worker and a Christian. I told Randy my mom would be mad if I even approached her about the issue of his arms.

However, Randy insisted I ask. So one day after church while Mom and I were in the kitchen, I asked what her reaction would be if Randy and I were thinking about getting married. I also asked if his disability would bother her.

She stopped what she was doing, stared at me very indignantly, and said, "Well, no, of course not. All we ever asked was that you marry a faithful Christian and hard worker. Randy is definitely both of those. Why would the issue of his arms bother me?" Then she said she and Dad had been watching us and knew we were in love.

Mom had always said, "When you meet the right person, you will know. " I really had the feeling Randy was the right person. When I heard my mom say she and Dad completely accepted Randy that was that. She said it seemed to her Randy and I were made for each other.

In January, Randy drove out to Lubbock to ask my dad's permission to marry me. Then Randy took me out to dinner and asked me to marry him. I said yes. During Valentine's Day, 1974, we were at a conference in Dallas with Chet Reames, state director of BSU for Texas. We told him we were engaged and asked him to perform the wedding ceremony.

That night we announced our engagement to the whole group. People really liked Randy. Not one person said anything about him not having arms. They may have been thinking something. However, Randy was so popular, no one said a word.

Later on, one girl I knew really well did ask me some personal questions. She asked if I had thought about "certain things" and had I considered whether or not we could have a "marriage relationship." I told her, "Randy and I have talked and all he's missing is his arms."

She also asked me something interesting: How did I feel about the fact I wouldn't be hugged? I told her Randy had part of one arm, so he could hug. But I believed then, and I still believe now, that the concept of wholeness involves what's on the inside.

Everyone has problems. There are lots of people who appear fine on the outside, but then they go and jump off a bridge or blow their brains out. People can have all their body parts and not be whole on the inside. People can be mentally ill and have all their body parts. Yet, if they were being honest, they would tell you they aren't whole. They know.

Randy may have artificial arms, but he is the most "whole" person I have ever met. Randy is so whole he is able to help and lead other people to wholeness. That's what he does. I was attracted to his wholeness. In a lot of ways, he is more whole than I am. I am shy and still afraid to be around people. I would rather stay in the background, which keeps me from developing my leadership potential. Wholeness comes from who we are on the inside. There is a journey to wholeness and God grows us, if we let Him. The more we know who we are in Christ, the more whole we become.

I recently turned sixty and the profoundness of life is that it's a journey. No one should give up or take shortcuts. I tell young people who want to get married to not do it too quickly. Oswald Chambers, in his devotional book, "My Utmost for His Highest", wrote that we can be tempted to take a shortcut to get to our highest goal. He warned that the shortcut may keep us from finding the right pathway to our ultimate goal. Pray God will bring the right person into your life at the right time.

Many pastors teach that God has a good and perfect will for our lives, which is true. But I believe Satan has a plan for your life as well. It's a terrible plan. He will come in and tempt you with the wrong husband or wife. Wait for God's best. This belief comes in large part from personal experience. See, there was a time before Randy came along when I was tempted with a marriage choice. It wouldn't have been God's best for my life. I had actually been engaged in 1973 to another guy. This was before I knew Randy.

One day I realized this was not the type of person I was supposed to marry. He didn't fit the description of the person that I knew in my heart was God's best for me. I said yes because he kept asking, not because I loved him. I got tired of saying no. Finally, we broke up. That was just a very short while before I met Randy.

Several months later, while Randy and I were dating long distance, this young man came back and said he wanted to take me in his car to show me something. What he showed me was that he had bought me a house. Again he asked me to marry him. I told him it was a very nice house. I also told him I knew who I was going to marry, and it wasn't him. He needed to go out and find the right person for him. I found my unique and different person in Randy.

When I think about life, I think of those wooden frame puzzles you see preschoolers playing with. We see the outline, the frame. God slowly adds pieces to the puzzle of our lives. We can't see the whole picture, even when we are twenty or so. We see the frame and a piece or two. It's important to let God add the pieces in His timing.

Chapter 14

THE WORKAHOLIC

Randy

As I said, I had a lot of trepidation about my relationship with Mary Ann because of a lack of good marriage role models. But Mary Ann stuck with me. Her mom was developing a large home health care business in West Texas. Her dad worked for the Texas Employment Commission. He listened to unemployment claims forty hours a week, year after year. Many of the claims were from people who didn't want to work. They always had an excuse for not being able to find or keep a job. Then he saw me – a guy with two artificial arms who was working his heart out – active, and going all over the state. I had every excuse not to work, but I was working as hard as I knew how. He liked that.

I learned that Mary Ann's dad had also wanted to be a minister when he was young. I was getting to do what he wanted to do; serve the Lord through full-time ministry. Her dad was also a deacon and a Sunday school teacher. They had actually helped start Southcrest Baptist Church in Lubbock. Southcrest has grown to be one of the largest, most active churches in the nation.

Her parents admired the fact I had gumption, was tough, and had zeal. They didn't mind the artificial arms. So I officially asked

her to marry me on Valentine's Day, 1975, at a BSU conference at
Cliff Temple Baptist Church in Dallas. When she said yes, I was
elated. That really lit up the conference for me.

I suppose I should explain that after the extra semester of traveling around, my boss called and asked if I was going to seminary or back into engineering. I really wanted to go to seminary
because I felt God was steering me in that direction. The people
at the state BSU office asked me how I planned to get through
seminary. What was I going to do for money? I said I planned to
get a part-time engineering job. They said a BSU position at two
community colleges in Dallas had just opened up. They invited me
for an interview.

At the interview I learned that if I accepted the job, I could
only go to seminary part time. That meant it would take a little longer to get through. However, for a part-time job, it paid
pretty well. The job would require me to live in Dallas, which was
thirty miles away from the seminary. But I discovered a group
of college friends who were living in Dallas and were carpooling to seminary each day. I would make the fourth person, and
we'd each drive one day a week. That cut the commuting costs by
three-fourths.

I prayed a lot and interviewed for the BSU job. Two or three
days after the interview, I got a call that I'd been chosen. Most
guys who worked in a college like this began in the fall and worked
through the spring. This job opening began in January. That was
really unusual, but it worked out great for me. I could be there in
January and get things started for the new semester.

I started as the BSU director for El Centro and Mountain
View colleges in December. That happened right as I completed
my semester of traveling to the twenty-eight campuses around the
state. The previous BSU director had an office at Cliff Temple

Baptist Church, and they allowed me to keep the office. The folks at Cliff Temple really loved me and I loved them.

When Mary Ann and I got married, we joined a class for newlyweds and young marrieds at the church. Those folks have always been very good to us and still are to this day. Mary Ann and I were involved in the church. I was involved in BSU at two campuses and I was attending seminary. Needless to say, we were really busy.

My belief was, and still is, that discipleship is the way to reach the world for Christ. BSU was a place within the Christian structure to spread discipleship quickly. On a campus, you can reach a lot of people. Those two community colleges where I worked became places to experiment with different ways of transforming lives. We wanted to find the most effective ways to show students how much God loved them, and how much we cared. I started some evangelism projects and noontime lunches. Everything I'd ever seen was tried at those two schools.

Entering seminary was everything I had hoped it would be; an incredible experience. One of my professors was the renowned theologian William L Hendricks. He was the person who said, "When you cannot agree upon truth, then lean into goodness and learn from beauty so you can approach truth in a new way." Dr. Hendricks wrote "A Theology for Children" and was a brilliant scholar.

Another professor was Dr. David Fite. He had been arrested in Cuba in the 1960s for sharing the Gospel of Jesus Christ. He ended up serving several years in prison there. Dr. Fite heard my first sermon and after that he called me aside. He wanted to know what my plans were after I graduated from seminary.

I told him I was planning to continue working with college students. He said, "You can preach. Some fellows enter student work because they fear preaching, but you can preach." Up to that point, I had really just worked off my testimony when I spoke. His words were a real confidence builder for me, and a real blessing. Being at Southwestern Seminary from 1974 to 1978 was an amazing experience. The caliber of professors and the commitment they had to their students had a lifelong impact on me.

Being a newlywed, working at two college campuses in Dallas, and attending seminary in Fort Worth took all the organizational skills I could muster. I would get up at 5:30 a.m. and meet the other guys I was carpooling with at 6:30. We'd meet at a designated spot and be at seminary by 7:25. There were two hours of classes and then we would head back to Dallas to work all day. One of the guys worked at a church and the rest of us worked on college campuses.

It was interesting to see the change in myself during those years. I had gone from being a real introvert to being someone who really needed to be around people. The people person within me was unleashed and the engineer/scholar who was studying theology took something of a backseat. My grades were all A's and B's. I did okay in seminary, but if I had it to do over again, I would spend a lot more time in Greek and Hebrew.

The fact was that I was a workaholic who was fed by being around other people. I'd be on campus at El Centro and Mountain View five days a week; whereas the other guys doing campus work at community colleges were only on their campuses three days a week. When I first started seminary, the registrar said it would be tempting to sideline my graduate work. He warned against it, saying the training I received would serve me my entire life.

I was trying to keep up with my studies, working on them from the time I got home until midnight. Then I'd be up again at 5:30 to head to Fort Worth for classes. I was also leading retreats two or three weekends a month. And keep in mind that I was now married. Mary Ann would say, "You're going to kill yourself. Nobody can do this much without rest."

I'd argue it was God's will and a great opportunity. Mary Ann finally got me to see the value of rest and pacing myself enough to just do one retreat a month. I'd have the other three weekends to go to church, study, get rest, and do things with Mary Ann and other young married couples. Her advice probably saved both my life and my marriage.

One morning I got up and was so tired, I missed the car pool. I had to drive over to Fort Worth by myself. On the way home, I fell asleep on Interstate 30. I was awakened by the sound of the tires hitting the side of the road. That was the final straw; I couldn't keep burning the candle on both ends. I had to listen to Mary Ann and get more rest.

In spite of that, the campus work was continuing to grow and bear fruit. We had meetings at one campus on Tuesday nights and at the other one on Thursday nights. It wasn't work for the sake of work. It was reaching people with the message of Jesus Christ, then helping them grow in their faith and equipping them to share their faith with others.

So what came next seemed like a crisis. The BSU decided to divide up the area, cut our pay, and hire twice as many directors. Suddenly I wasn't going to have a way to pay the bills or take care of Mary Ann. We prayed hard for an answer from God. Shortly afterward, a dentist who attended our church stepped forward to help. Mary Ann was attending nursing school and I was in seminary. The dentist asked us to figure out what it was going to cost to commute to seminary each day and convey that information to the church office.

She gave the church a gift in that amount for them to give to us. Even though I was taking a pay cut from the BSU, God immediately covered the amount through a scholarship I received, along with the dentist's grant through the church to pay for gasoline and tuition.

Chapter 15

DISABILITY OR INCONVENIENCE?

Mary Ann

When I was a little girl, I became interested in how my dad tied his tie. I asked him to show me how he did it. He said okay, but that he only knew how to tie it on himself. I watched him tie that tie until I could do it standing in front of him. There's a big difference in tying a tie on yourself and doing it on someone else.

Even though I was only six at the time, I had never forgotten how to tie that tie. You might think that's an unusual thing for a child of six to be interested in or to remember. It turned out I married a guy with no hands who often needed to wear a tie. I've now been standing in front of Randy for almost forty years tying his tie.

People wonder what it's like being handicapped or being married to a handicapped person. What Randy would tell you is he can pretty much do what everyone else can do. It just takes him a little longer to do it and it's inconvenient. Randy was speaking to a group of sixth graders one time and they asked all these questions adults would never ask.

One of them was, "How do you take a shower?" He told them he takes a pail of soapy water into the shower along with a towel.

He has just enough arm to be able to pick up the towel and sling it around with the soapy water so he gets washed. The kids laughed and said it sounded like a battle in the shower. Then Randy rinses off and gets out. Once he gets out, he has another battle with a dry towel. He slings it around until he gets dried off.

A few years ago, we were at a Christian conference on disabilities in Waco, Texas. Ken Medema, a very popular Christian singer/ songwriter who happens to be blind, was also there. Randy was speaking and Ken was doing the music. I was standing back stage with Ken's wife and she said, "I don't know if I could be married to a guy with Randy's disabilities."

I told her I wouldn't have been prepared to marry a guy who was blind. What we realized was that when people think of marrying a disabled person, their mind plays a trick on them. They think of marrying a person with every disability. You don't marry the whole world of disabilities. You marry someone who has a specific situation or situations. And most of the disabilities the world contends with aren't physical. Most disabilities can't be seen by the naked eye.

The beauty of marriage is that it's all about helping with things that are hard for the other person. The things they can do well, you leave them alone about. I do the bills in our house. Why? I'm a more analytical thinker and I actually enjoy it. But there's another reason, too. Opening envelopes is a pain when you don't have hands. Randy could do it, but dealing with all the envelopes and stamps would take him ten times longer.

About the time Randy and I got married, God used my parents to again help me see the importance of accepting different people. My brother, Mike, was one of the original hippies, even though we were from conservative Lubbock. He moved to Fort Worth and started a business hiring young people to sell carnations on street corners. It was the era of "peace, love, and flower power."

Mike had a girlfriend named Sherry who came out of a very hard life. She got pregnant at seventeen and had a little boy. We met Sherry and her little boy, Eric, when Eric was two and a half. My parents accepted them. Sherry eventually broke up with my brother when Eric was five. Sherry tried life on her own, but it was just too hard. She couldn't make enough money to get by.

Even after Sherry and my brother broke up, Mom said, "If you ever decide you want to go back to school and get your education, we will help you."

How? My mom and dad invited Sherry and Eric to come live with them. Mom and Dad would put Sherry through nursing school. Who would do that for their son's ex-girlfriend? So in August of 1975, Sherry and five-year-old Eric went to live with my parents in Lubbock. For the next three years, my parents put her through school so she could get her licensed vocational nurses degree. My mother also took in Charlie, her Down's syndrome brother. He lived with them for twenty years.

Sherry ended up marrying a pilot from Reese Air Force Base near Lubbock. From 1975 until the day my parents died, they treated Sherry like their daughter. I still call her my foster sister. I watched my parents "adopt" a twenty-one year old and her child. I was twenty-two at the time. It was really neat.

Sherry and Eric needed help and my parents helped them. But it wasn't just "help them and then move on." It was adopting them into the family. That was an incredible example to me. It is a picture of what Jesus Christ does for us when we are adopted into the family of God.

One time, Sherry said to me, "In the three years I lived with your parents, they taught me more about good parenting and how to love people than my own biological parents did in my entire life." In the New Testament of the Bible, in James 1:7, it says that religion that is pure is taking care of widows and orphans and refusing to be corrupted by the world. The Bible also teaches that our relationship with Christ is through a spiritual adoption. We are adopted into the family of God as His child through Jesus Christ. So the idea of adoption runs deep all through scripture.

If we are Christians, we are adopted into the Family of Faith. We are joint heirs with Christ, even though we're adopted. There are no step-children in Christianity. We are all full members of the family. Of course, those scriptural truths were in the Bible long before Sherry and her little boy, Eric, came along. But my parents lived them out. Eric is now grown, married, and has children of his own.

Back to my marriage with Randy, the biggest challenge in being married to him wasn't dealing with his disabilities. It was his almost ceaseless energy. It was a real challenge getting him to see the importance of slowing down and resting. I told him he had to slow down or he was going to kill himself. He did eventually slow down...a little bit.

Chapter 16

HAPPY EMERGENCIES

Randy

Back in December 1973, while we were still in Texas, an amazing person named Henry Blackaby came down from Canada to speak at student meetings and retreats. He's the one who later wrote *Experiencing God,* which is one of the great books on discipleship. He talked to us about stepping out in faith and all the amazing things God could do when we trusted Him. Henry ended up playing a major role in our lives as a close friend and a mentor. We saw Henry several times over the years. Mary Ann even had a friend who moved to Canada to work with Henry. In the meantime I graduated from seminary and Mary Ann added a degree in nursing to her résumé.

Our commitment was to always serve God where we were needed most. During the spring I had explored a job possibility in California. They contacted me and asked me to consider taking a job developing student work on campuses around Riverside, California. I was also contacted about student work in Florida and Texas. The one that seemed the least developed and most in need of what we could provide was the position in California. We prayed and God really gave us a heart for that area. Interestingly, this was within a few miles of where I'd gone to get physical therapy and my first set of artificial arms eleven years earlier. It was also near where Mary Ann had done her summer mission work in East L.A.

It was funny, because I hadn't sought any of these jobs. People approached me. I didn't even have a résumé, but doors kept opening. That's God at work. I guess you could say we were being carried along by the Holy Spirit. It was more or less, "Just say yes, you will follow, or no you won't." The very things these campuses needed in a leader were the things God had given to me. So it really was a phenomenal time of seeing what God can do if we will just have faith and be obedient.

We became convinced California was the place God wanted us to serve. I would be the area student minister, as well as campus minister for California Baptist College, now California Baptist University, which only had about six hundred students back then. When we arrived in California, the people at Cal Baptist asked Mary Ann what she planned to do. She had just graduated from nursing school, so she thought she would probably get a nursing job somewhere.

The college ended up hiring her to be the director of health services on campus, so that worked out great. It had been a part-time position, but they bumped it up to full time. She also got a chance to teach two intro health courses on campus. Preparing for those classes and teaching fifty freshmen four times a week developed her in some wonderful ways. Mary Ann became more and more comfortable being in front of people. She ended up spending eight years teaching in the classroom. It was also a time for us to continue learning what it meant to be a married couple.

Meanwhile, I was getting to know many of the churches and pastors in the area and developing the student ministry. It was a high-pressure eight years. There were twenty-one college campuses in the metropolitan area. The first year I really just focused on developing my ministry at Cal Baptist. Next I wanted to seize the opportunity to create new ministries on the other area campuses. This meant I had to find volunteers and train workers for those campuses. I found willing students and key pastors and worked from the base at California Baptist to reach seven state universities. We had retreats and fellowships to get students from various campuses together and to have bigger events than any single campus could sponsor on their own.

In some ways, working in California was a big cultural change for us. It took some time to adjust to the differences in culture between Texas and California. There seemed to be much more of an emphasis on your choices of recreation: parties, going to the beach, the Disneyland mentality.

In Texas, one of the first questions people ask you is, "What do you do for a living?" In California, I don't think one person asked me that. Californians wanted to know what my hobbies were. They'd ask, "So, what are you into?" They didn't care what I did for a living. It was all about what I enjoyed on the weekend. They wanted to know, "Are you a skater or a surfer or a biker or a snow skier?" That was an adjustment, but for someone who struggles with being a workaholic, it was a good adjustment. It helped me relax and enjoy weekends more. Life became more than work.

On the home front, Mary Ann and I knew we didn't have enough money to have children while we were both in graduate school. So we waited. When we did try to have children, it didn't happen. Why? I don't know. Maybe somehow I'd been damaged by all the medicines and anesthetics during the thirty-eight surgeries. Mary Ann had also been on arthritis medication for gout since she was thirteen. Whatever the reason, the end result was Mary Ann didn't get pregnant.

She had read books on adopting and wanted to adopt since she was very young. So we decided to apply to adopt a child and leave it in God's hands. We came to the conclusion if we were going to add to our family, we would add through adoption. We registered with the county-sponsored adoption agency because we couldn't afford private adoption. Riverside County, California, had classes, adoption fairs, and all kinds of things to encourage adoption. We were told the waiting period for a baby was seven years. That's a long time to wait. We thought we might help other children in the meantime through foster parenting. We got two teenagers.

Unfortunately, these two teens were seasoned at working the system. They had been in children's homes and foster care all their lives. They knew how to play the game. We were young and idealistic. They played the game all over us. Someone told us, "The book on parenting comes in two volumes. You started in volume two."

We worked with that situation for several years, but realized being foster parents of teens just wasn't for us. It probably would have been different if we had started with younger children. We absolutely encourage people to be foster parents if that's their calling. But they also need to go into it with their eyes open. We wanted to fix these kids' problems, but we couldn't. It also turned out these two really wanted to be in the children's home environment rather than with a family.

In 1984, after the period with the foster children, we needed a break. We went up to Alaska to see Sherry, Mary Ann's "foster sister." We let Henry Blackaby know we were coming up that way. At the time, Henry was the director of missions in Vancouver, British Columbia. He and his wife invited us to stay at their house while we were in Vancouver. It was an exciting time because Henry was getting ready for an international event called Expo 86.

Mary Ann

I had known since I was twelve that one day I would adopt children. I was never one to have that overwhelming drive to give birth, but I always wanted to adopt. We first tried being foster parents for a brother and sister. Unfortunately, they came to us with a lot of emotional problems and that didn't go very well.

The year we applied to adopt, they told us there was a five to seven year waiting list. The previous year, only five percent of infants conceived outside of marriage were placed for adoption. Ninety-five percent were either aborted or kept by a single parent. This was a time when agencies tried to put children with a family of the same ethnicity. There were only twelve Anglo children adopted the previous year out of a county with a population of two million people.

Really, the door to adoption should have been closed to us. That's because of the rules they had in place regarding the ages of the adopting parents. We had the two children from foster care for two years. Then we had a year with no children. The foster children had been a really stressful period, but we still wanted a baby. We took the year off to work through all of that.

Randy was technically a year too old to adopt a baby, but the county said, "Your file was left open from when you first applied" – that was before we were foster parents – "so technically, you are still within the age range." That was a miracle.

Randy

In August of 1984, we got a call that they had a baby for us. It turned out the wait was only five years instead of seven. The birth mom had requested several things that the state was obligated to try to fulfill. In California, birth moms can request some pretty peculiar things. What this birth mom requested that moved us way up on the list was a Christian family that didn't drink alcohol.

Because of my dad's drinking and Mary Ann's upbringing, neither one of us drank. That meant we skipped ahead several years on that list of two hundred-plus families. It turned out we were the only Christian, non-drinking family on the list. When the county called, we were at Glorieta, New Mexico, at a Christian retreat center. We actually took groups to Glorieta for twenty-one straight years. This call came during one of those times.

When the adoption people called, they told the switchboard operator they had to talk to us because there was a "happy emergency." We returned the call and they said if we wanted him, there was a three-week old baby boy, ten pounds and growing like a weed.

They said we needed to get on a plane and get back to California. And boy oh boy, we did! We got him the next Monday morning. His name is John Mark Gallaway. He was born while the 1984 Olympics were going on in Los Angeles, which is right next door to where we lived in Riverside.

We would have gotten him at birth, instead of three weeks later, but many officials who had to sign off on the adoption were attending the Olympics. Therefore, they had trouble getting a quorum together of the people to approve it.

Mary Ann

There were two hundred parents waiting for adoptions when we got John. God could have given him to any one of them. (It helped us to remember that later when he went through his teenage years.) I really have a lot of respect for birth mothers who place their children for adoption. They give a child two great gifts. The first is life. The second is that they realize they are not in a position to take care of the child, so they give him or her to a family who can. John's birth mother was sixteen years old and not married.

The first night we had John, he woke up at midnight and stayed up until three a.m. That's the night we bonded, while Randy was asleep. It was like, "Hey, you are really mine." We got John and we thought, "Wow, this is good." John ate every three or four hours for the first few months of his life. He was an easy baby as soon as we got used to being sleep deprived.

Let me add that a lot of people don't think staying at home and raising children is hard work. It is a lot of work, but very important. Looking back on it after all these years, I see that being at home with the children was even more important than I realized at the time. You are molding someone to become a productive citizen, helping to impart character traits into them. When young mothers get frustrated, I remind them that what they are going through is only one of many seasons in life. This will only be a fifteen- or sixteen-year window out of a sixty or seventy year life.

So Randy was a BSU director in Southern California, and I was the school nurse and taught the freshman health classes. There was another couple who were our friends. They had a child about John's age and were pregnant with their second. I thought it would also be a good time for us to have another child, too. One day I mentioned in class about our desire to adopt again. I asked if anyone knew of someone who was pregnant and was already planning to place their baby for adoption. Sure enough, one of the students knew of a friend who had gotten pregnant and didn't want to abort but wasn't in a position to keep the baby.

That girl was due on March 27, but had the baby on March 20. The adoption was put on the fast track because we had been planning on going to Canada to do mission work. It's almost unheard of, but the adoption was all finalized in four months. In California, adoptions were never formally finalized until the child was twelve months old. We knew that and had told the Lord we would just stay and work in California until He was ready for us to go to Canada. We would know because that would be when the adoption went through. Our second child, Amy, was born in 1986. Her adoption was tied on to Johns'. It was a piggyback adoption, which meant they waved the adoption fee on the second child. We almost couldn't believe it.

Randy

Mary Ann told the students in her health classes all about adoption. She said to the students if they knew of anyone, for whatever reason, who needed to use adoption, we were interested in adopting. The message was, "Don't abort! There are good, loving families who desperately want to have children and can't. At least contact an adoption agency and consider the possibility." I said, "Young ladies, give your babies a family, not a funeral."

One of the things Mary Ann said was, "You might save a baby's life if you tell people about the adoption option." There was a girl in Mary Ann's class, a girl she didn't even think was paying attention, who went home over a break, found an old high school friend who had gotten pregnant, and shared the news. It was the girl's pastor who called us to see if we were really interested.

We said, "Of course we're interested." One of the benefits of private adoption is you have the option to meet the birth mom while she's still pregnant. We met this young lady a month before the birth, so she could have peace with us being the parents of her future child. The process rolled along really quickly and we got the newborn, who we named Amy Nicole Gallaway, in 1986.

Mary Ann

One thing to make clear is that John and Amy *are not* our "adopted children." They are our children. Sometimes people who are adopted struggle with the idea that someone gave them up. You hear about people who really have a hard time with that.

What I like to remind people in those situations is, "Your biological parents gave you two great gifts. They gave you life, and they gave you a family. Then, at some point, people have to decide where to place their focus. Are they going to focus on that they were given up or that they were taken in?"

One of the first big issues adoptive parents face is the where-did-I-come-from stage when children are four or five. I had prayed the Lord would prepare me for that day. We found a book called *God Made My Family* by Felicity Henderson that really helped.

It didn't say anything about going to the hospital like a lot of baby books did. I read that book to my kids when they were little. When John was four, a lady from our church was seven months pregnant. Everyone was talking about it. John was riding his tricycle around at home one day. Suddenly he stops and says, "Mom, you were there when I was born, right?"

I told him, "No, I wasn't there." I explained there was a special place inside mommies where babies grow. "Mommy's special place didn't work right," I told him, "so God had you grow inside another lady. But all the time, He knew you were going to be our baby." I explained how we got him at three weeks old and he was okay with that.

Later, when Randy got home, John ran to meet him. He said, "Daddy, mommy's 'grow place' is broken. So I grew inside somebody else! Do you want to play?" So that's how John first came across the concept he was adopted.

When John was in first grade, he had a teacher from Quebec who had a really long last name that was hard to pronounce. Everyone just called her Miss Terry Anne. She got pregnant in September. She had twin girls in March. He talked all about it. Amy had the same teacher two years later and Miss Terry Anne was pregnant again. When the teacher had the baby and was out on maternity leave, that's when the concept of adoption really began to dawn on Amy.

She wondered about the idea that her birth mother gave her away or "gave her up," as many people say. I hate those terms. We have to help kids cope with that kind of wording. Unfortunate terms like "your birth mother gave you away" are very hurtful. As I said earlier, adopted children can focus on that or on the fact their adoptive parents went through all the processes – years of paperwork and interviews and so forth – to have them come into their lives.

Adoption is such a wonderful way for families to bring a child into their homes. You fill out reams of paperwork. Then, after years of waiting, out of the blue you receive a phone call from someone who says, "We have a child for you."

Then the prospective parents walk into a room at a hospital or orphanage. Someone brings in a child and says, "This child can be yours." At that moment, the prospective parents have a choice to make. Then they open their heart and choose to love.

All children deserve to be loved by caring adults. In my opinion, a big part of having a great family heritage means you have been loved deeply by someone in your life. We prayed for six years to adopt children. God moved in many ways for us to be able to adopt the two children that we adopted. We love John and Amy so much.

Chapter 17

CANADA CALLING

Randy

I had been admitted to Golden Gate Seminary outside San Francisco and was starting work on my doctorate. Attending Golden Gate Seminary had been based on a desire to learn more about servant leadership, Christian organizations, and theology. Two men I really admired, Dr. Bill Pinson and Dr. Bill Hendricks from Southwestern Seminary in Fort Worth, were out there.

Dr. Hendricks was such a creative thinker, knew seven different languages, and was a real inspiration. He also had a great sense of humor. He would say things like, "I am so tired of students with the bodies of whales and the minds of minnows." What I remember most about Dr. Pinson is he could articulate the theology of the entire world's major religions so eloquently.

At most seminaries the doctoral programs are field based. The program is designed for people who are already in professional ministry and don't have the leisure of taking three years off to study. It is set up to have a local committee that oversees your work. Then you go to the seminary campus every few months for eight to ten days of intensive seminars.

There are professors who do testing, analysis of your strengths and weaknesses, etc. It is a personal, professional growth experience over two or three years. You also do a practicum. A PhD is more theoretical. What I earned, a Doctorate of Ministry, is more field based.

When it was time to attend a seminar at Golden Gate, I would leave Riverside and drive three hundred and fifty miles to San Francisco. For eight to ten days I would stay in one of the dorms on campus, and then would go home and study and absorb. Then the process would start over again.

One of the things of which I became most aware was how Jesus would disciple men. He trained through a visionary challenge, significant amounts of time and association, and then gave assignments. There would then be reflection and feedback when they returned.

Jesus cast a vision, gave a calling, and gathered the twelve disciples. They were with Him day and night for three years. They saw how He dealt with the helpless, the homeless, the Romans, the religious leaders, and every kind of adversity. After that, in Matthew 10 and Luke 10, He sent them out. They reported back and then Jesus helped them solidify in their minds the takeaway lessons.

Roger Coleman, in *The Master Plan of Evangelism*, talked a lot about this. I saw this change my life. I worked to follow that model in the student work I did. Coleman said passing on what is in you to others happens through an eight-step process: 1. Selection of the right people. 2. A deep, meaningful association with them. 3. Putting your blessing on their work. 4. Equipping them not only with what you know, but with who you are. 5. Demonstration of key principles and methods. 6. Delegation of authority. 7. Supervision. 8. Reproducing yourself in this person so they can carry on after you.

Whether you are working on machinery or doing sales, or evangelism, or whatever, this gives us a plan for how to do that.

After my orientation for the doctorate, I was invited up to Edmonton to speak. We became acquainted with the wonderful Canadian winters and delightful Canadian people. Mary Ann had always wanted to live someplace where it got really cold and snowy in the winter. Canada was it.

While I was attending seminary at Golden Gate, Canada was always in the back of our minds. We knew it was the right place for us, but not the right time. It's very important when God is calling you that you not only go *where* He is calling, but *when* He is calling. Many times He places a call on your life. You may even know where He wants you to be. But it might not be time yet. The *who* and the *where* might be revealed, but the *when* is still sometime in the future. However, He is still preparing you.

During my time in seminary, I also met several people from Canada. They were telling us about the needs there. We also continued our relationship with Henry Blackaby, who was preparing for an event called Expo 86. Further, he wanted us to come and to bring a team of college students to help out.

Mary Ann

In 1986, we decided we were being called to Canada. It was the right place, right time. At that point, Henry and Marilynn Blackaby were heavily involved in getting ready for Expo 86. In February of 1986 when we were preparing for Expo, we got the call to adopt Amy. She came into the picture in March. When Randy left for Expo, I had a twenty-two-month-old son and a two-month-old daughter.

I wanted to go to Expo because it would have been exciting. At first I was wishing like crazy I could go. However, with a toddler and an infant, what I needed to do was stay home with the kids. I was on a new journey of motherhood. As all new parents learn, my priorities had shifted so that I was excited to stay home with our babies.

While I was taking care of our children, I was also praying for Randy and the group. Randy called when he could to give me updates. A girl named Gina was also on my mind. She was one of the students in Randy's group. She signed up to go on the trip and then almost backed out. I was so glad she went. We believe very strongly that if you have an opportunity to do something unique, do it. So we were very glad Gina decided to go. I'm a very strong introvert, but that philosophy has helped me be courageous and get out of my shell. If I hadn't had that philosophy, there were so many great opportunities I would have missed. I felt the same way about Gina and was praying she would see this as a life-changing event.

Even though I was at home, it was important to pray for Randy and the team that was up in Vancouver. I knew they would run into people who, when they heard the word Christian, had all different ideas of what that meant. The essence of Christianity involves knowing there's a God who loves me beyond my wildest dreams. He cares about me, encourages me, and offers forgiveness for my sins through Jesus. He's always there for me. I want others to have the opportunity to hear about Him and make their own choice. In the book of First Peter it says that we are to quietly trust our lives to God. Then if anyone asks us the reason we believe, tell them, but in a gentle and respectful way. That was my prayer for the team.

When I pray, I know that God is right here in the room. I can ask Him to help me. I communicate with Him the same way I would a dear, trusted friend. I can ask Him to help other people, too. Of course, He's God. It's His choice what He does. He controls the universe and He can see millions of years in any direction. He knows what's coming next and what's best in a situation. Prayer isn't about getting God's attention. The Christian has God's attention. He's a listening God who cares about me; who cares about everybody.

Randy

The full name of Expo 86 was The 1986 World Exposition on Transportation and Communication. It was a huge World's Fair that featured pavilions sponsored by fifty-four nations and which lasted for six months. It was a time when hundreds of thousands of people from all over the world would converge on Vancouver. In other words, it was a great time to tell lots of different people about Jesus and have a worldwide impact on people's lives.

We took twenty-one college students from California up to Expo 86 to help out. Our primary focus was walking around meeting people at exhibits. We were learning about people from all over the world and what their needs were. We learned a lot about different cultures. We were there for two weeks meeting people, praying with them if they desired that, and planting seeds of faith through relationships.

The students stayed in Christian homes in the Vancouver area. We encouraged our students to be keen observers and try to determine where others were in their spiritual journey. In Canada, the idea that people can believe whatever they want as long as they keep it to themselves is sometimes promoted as tolerance.

As evangelicals, our rationale for sharing what we've discovered is based on the fact we see so many people who don't know which way to turn. They don't know how to solve their problems. Therefore, the kind and generous thing to do is to share the answer we've found. We should at least give others a chance to know Jesus.

I have found an answer to life's problems in the person of Jesus Christ. It's incumbent on me to at least offer a relationship with Him to others. They can decline, but at least they know He's there for them. Think of it this way: If someone is on the side of the road with a flat tire and they can't go on, but I know how to change a tire and can help them, isn't it right to stop and offer to help?

Christians didn't invent the answer. We were lost and someone shared Christ with us. So now we are sharing Christ with others who are still looking for the answer to life, the meaning of life. That's what I was doing in California and it's what I was teaching the students to do during our time in Vancouver.

One way to think about the Christian desire to share our faith is this: Can you imagine if someone knew there was a vaccine against small pox or polio, but they didn't tell anyone? No one is obligated to take the vaccine, but don't we have an obligation to tell them about it? How would someone feel if they contracted a vaccine-preventable disease and then found out about the vaccine, but only after they were dying of the disease? That would be a tragedy.

Christians shouldn't try to push anybody to become a believer. In fact, if I could magically make someone become a Christian, I wouldn't do it. I want them to be aware and then decide for themselves. Expo 86 was that opportunity to share with others, to make them aware. We were there to help them see that Christians aren't people to be afraid of, but to know we cared about them. We were also letting people know there is a vaccine that prevents eternal separation from God, and it's free.

Let me tell you about one of the students who went on the trip with us and how it changed her life. When we were getting ready to go, we began publicizing the trip to the students with whom I worked. One day I was in my office and talking to some students about going to Canada to Expo 86. A delightful young lady named Gina came in. She sang in one of the college music groups we had. She was pretty, sociable, kind. She had a very high speaking voice, but when she sang, it was with the voice of an angel. She was wavering about whether she should go to Expo 86 or stay home.

I said to her something I say to people still. "Gina, if you stay home, two weeks will go by and, ten years from now, you probably won't even remember what you did in those two weeks. In fact, you probably won't even remember in a year. Life will just go by, filled with the normal, everyday things you do. But if you go on this trip with us, there are all kinds of possibilities that come with meeting new people, seeing a new country, maybe even meeting people attending the world's fair from countries you've never heard of. You'll be making memories that I guarantee you'll still carry ten years from now."

She heard me say that several times and finally decided to go. On that trip, she met Mel Blackaby. Mel is one of Henry Blackaby's four sons. Henry was one of the key Christian leaders in Vancouver. Mel was a tall, handsome fellow with a brilliant mind who later got a PhD. Mel and Gina met, were attracted to each other, and fell in love. That started a long-distance romance for them and eventually they got married. Today they have several children and a dynamic life together. Had Gina not taken that path of adventure and gone to Vancouver, she might have never met that young man.

The group was so excited to go up to Vancouver. It was glorious weather. The city was so beautiful with the flowers and the shimmering blue water. It was like landing in the Garden of Eden. Henry Blackaby found host families who would put us up in their homes. The momentum and thrill of the world coming together, of all these volunteers greeting people and welcoming the world, was exhilarating. The churches hosted volunteers, hundreds of them, from all over America and Canada. We did community events and helped the churches staff different venues. At night we would talk and pray with people. We would also share how Jesus had changed our lives.

For about a week we went up to visit the North Shore, a beautiful suburb of Vancouver. Our students went door to door. While I was up there, the national director for Southern Baptists of Canada, Allen Schmidt, drove up and down those streets trying to find me. He heard I might want to relocate to Canada and serve there. We sat down on a curb on one of those North Shore streets and talked about what the future might hold.

We were planting seeds of the Gospel. We were telling people from all over the world about Jesus. It was considered a great success. I understand a lot of businesses ended up locating in Vancouver because the city did such a great job hosting this event.

Coming from the smog of L.A., Vancouver was a literal breath of fresh air. For seven years I had been protected from the headaches and burning eyes of the pollution of L.A. But when God was moving us to Vancouver, suddenly the pollution started burning my eyes and I started getting headaches from all the smog.

Some people said we were crazy to leave Southern California and our secure jobs. We had retirement plans and healthcare. We were giving that up and moving to a position where we had to raise our own support. But we knew God was calling us to go. We filled out all the initial paperwork and they sent back an initial interview date. We went to the Canadian Consulate where we applied for Landed Immigrant Status, which is the same as permanent resident status here in the United States.

We told Henry Blackaby it was imperative to have Landed Immigrant Status instead of a temporary visa. We said, "If God is calling us, we aren't going to sell everything and then be asked by the government to leave in six months."

Henry wanted us to consider moving to Vancouver, not because of Expo 86, but because they needed someone doing student work up there. It would be the kind of work I had done in Texas and was now doing in California. They were looking for someone to coordinate student ministry on all the campuses and work with the churches, as well.

Chapter 18

HENRY BLACKABY AND EXTREME FAITH

Mary Ann

When I was a student at Texas Tech, Henry Blackaby was speaking at a lot of events. This was long before he wrote *Experiencing God*. I'm not sure when I first heard him, but he was showing up at a lot of different conferences.

We always went for a week to Glorieta in the summer and he spoke there, as well. He was a very quiet, dignified man who seemed to understand God and the Bible and could make it all come alive. He understood how to teach very deep concepts and could present them in very down-to-earth ways.

For example, he emphasized that God is always there and He isn't going to fail you. The more you read the Bible and know God's Word, and the more you live by the principles of the Bible, the more it comes alive in your life. He could teach the deep concepts of intimately knowing God.

Henry helped people know God's Word, live by it, and allow God to bless them. We loved hearing him speak. Randy was a speaker at some of those same conferences, but that was before he and I met. The other thing about Henry is he's such a gracious man.

As I think back, it's hard to remember a time when Henry Blackaby wasn't around, even though he was from Canada and we were in Texas. When Randy and I were engaged, some of the BSUs at the Dallas colleges got together and invited Henry to be the speaker for a weekend retreat. It was a small group, just two or three hundred people. We talked with Henry privately for an extended period. He really challenged us regarding the work God was doing in Canada.

When we moved to Southern California, we didn't realize Henry had a big connection there. Magnolia Avenue Baptist Church, which is where his in-law's Marilynn's parents, attended church, is literally right across the street from California Baptist College (now university). He would come down from Canada one or two times a year to see them. When he was in town, California Baptist College would invite him to speak on campus.

We had been in California about six years and Henry said, "I want you two to think about something. I want you to think about coming to Canada to work with me." When we first met him, he was working in Saskatchewan. He and Marilynn had four boys and a girl. The kids were like thirteen down to age five. He was there for years, and then moved to Vancouver to help the churches there.

He approached us about doing student ministries in Vancouver. They didn't have anyone doing that type of thing in the area. We promised to think and pray about it. This was during the period we were trying to adopt children. Henry asked us to come during the summer and see Vancouver. We went for a week and stayed at Henry and Marilynn's house. He showed us around and took us to the different college campuses. We also did the tourist things, seeing the incredible beauty, Vancouver Island, the gardens of Victoria, and all of that. We thought, "This is all very interesting. Maybe someday."

Before we left Vancouver, we made a trip to Simon Fraser University. Randy and I said, almost in unison, "This is the right place for us, but the wrong time." During the next two years we adopted John and Amy. When John was one, we agreed to go ahead and start the paperwork to move to Canada, with the idea of getting it turned in by September. Once the paperwork is turned in, they give you a hearing at the Canadian consulate in Los Angeles. It's a personal interview to see if they will let you into their country. Keep in mind, we were looking to move there, not just go as tourists.

About February tenth we got a call asking us if we wanted another child. We jumped at the chance. That was Amy. We knew we wanted her, but we were unsure how having a newborn might affect the process and the application.

Interestingly enough, the date for our interview with the embassy was March 26, 1986. That was the twentieth anniversary of the date Randy got electrocuted. He was kind of nervous about that day and all the memories it brought back. But it turned out to be amazing how God could take something so horrible and use it for good.

We lined up three babysitters for that time, so we had plenty of standbys in case something fell through with one of them. As it turned out, the first sitter's child got sick, so she couldn't help. The second sitter was sick herself. We actually had to use the third sitter.

When we got to the meeting at the Canadian consulate, the first question we were asked was, "Has anything changed in your family situation?"

Why yes, we have a six-day-old daughter! The lady was like, "Wow, you look amazing to have just had a baby six days ago!" We all had a good laugh and explained she was adopted. It turned out it was no problem at all. The lady with the embassy whipped out some forms and started filling them in. She said we were approved pending the finalization of the adoption of Amy. For very good reasons, you can't leave the United States and enter Canada with a child who doesn't have a passport. And you can't get a passport for an infant for whom you don't have legal custody.

At that point we knew once the adoption of Amy was complete, we would be moving to Canada. When we had first gone up there to see Henry and Marilynn Blackaby, I asked my mom how she would feel if we ever wanted to move up there. She said she had felt for a long time that one day we would be working with Henry. She said it would be a great place for them to visit if we did ever move. As I said before, I had felt since I was young that I would one day live in the west or northwest. We were already living in California, which was about as far west as you could go and not be in the ocean. Now we were feeling God moving us to the northwest.

Coming from Lubbock in the southwestern United States, where the nearest real mountains are in Colorado and New Mexico, I had always wanted to live somewhere that had a real winter. I love the snow and the cold. When it seemed like we might move to the Vancouver area, I was saying, "Okay, Lord! Okay!"

My parents were very practical about the whole thing and very committed to Jesus Christ. They believed you should listen to God and do what He directed you to do. So when we moved to California, it was, "Go! And go with our blessing. You go where you're supposed to go. Do what you feel the Lord is directing you to do."

The hardest part, when it actually came to moving to Canada, was leaving my job, which I loved. I had never been a full-time mom before and I didn't know how I would do in that role. I said to myself, "Okay, I will stay home for a couple of years and then go get a nursing job or a counselor job." I was working on my master's degree in clinical psychology prior to moving to Vancouver.

Randy actually moved to Vancouver in October and I didn't move until the first of December because I was finishing up two classes. Moving to a new country wasn't my only area of potential concern. I was about to be a full-time stay-at-home mom. How would I do at that? Also, being a real introvert, how would I do at meeting all these new people in a new situation? Other than the Blackabys and one other family, we didn't know anyone up there.

To be sure, when we moved, I felt very isolated and lonely. When you move like that, there are a million things to learn: new city, new people, new culture, being new parents, and learning what was expected of a minister's wife in that culture. It was all so new and different; very shaky and nerve racking for someone like me. Of course, the kids were too little to care, so they were fine.

Randy

I think Henry Blackaby is one of the most sincere, Godly men I've ever met. His knowledge of the Bible is extraordinary. He sees the hand of God at work. Part of the reason for the move to Canada was to be close to a great man of God and do something great for God. It's like D.L. Moody, the famous evangelist, said, "Expect great things from God and attempt great things for God."

I've always been an adventurer, willing to step out on faith. So the challenge of moving to Canada was really exciting. I know that some people have been disappointed after stepping out in faith, hoping God would sponsor their project. I think the secret is that if God is the one calling you to pursue a vision, then He will lead you to pray, seek good counsel, and explore the possibilities. He will also guide you to take wise steps of preparation. Scripture emphasizes that before we do anything, we should count the cost.

If all these components come together and your passion continues to grow, then you move forward. Once you are convinced it's God's will and you begin to move in that direction, God begins to move heaven and earth to confirm His assignment. Each time we have given up everything to go somewhere, God has come in the back door and blessed us even more than in our previous situation.

Sometimes in the journey, there was grief, and sometimes there was pain. But looking back, there were also times of incredible joy. Great faith was involved in moving to Canada because we had to raise our own support. When we accepted the position, we only had commitments for five hundred dollars per month. In a very real sense, it was crazy to move to Canada. Courage, foolishness, call it what you want. But we took this job with no salary and gave up two full-time jobs to do it.

We went as volunteers with a program called Mission Service Corps. We also had to go through Mission Service training. We never had to raise our own support before, so these were the Extreme Faith years. There are people who like the adrenaline rush of extreme sports. They ought to try Extreme Faith. Now that's an adrenaline rush.

When we resigned our jobs in Southern California, I had to take a break from my doctorate of ministry program. I couldn't raise the support to go to Canada, start new ministries, and finish my doctorate all at the same time. I had to take a year and a half leave of absence. However, I'm proud to say I did finish and graduate. Think about this: When we went, we didn't have our support in place. Further, anyone who knows Vancouver knows how hard it is to get a house there. And the houses you can get are very, very expensive.

Mary Ann

Marilynn Blackaby says when you cross the border into a developing nation, somewhere in Africa or South America, you immediately see the differences: the language issues, the poverty, and so forth. The longer you are there, the less you see the differences because you just begin to see them as people.

When you cross the border from the United States into Canada, it's just the opposite. It's, "Oh, we are all just exactly alike." In most of Canada people speak English, they look like Americans, etc. But the longer you are there, the more the differences come to light.

In America, the three bywords are Life, Liberty, and the Pursuit of Happiness. In Canada the bywords are Peace, Order, and Good Government, which comes from The Imperial Acts of Parliament. So how does that manifest itself? They are a quieter people. Another way it manifests itself becomes apparent when you look at the "two fences" theory.

That theory says everyone has two fences. Americans have a short outer fence. They will say hello, be friendly, talk about the weather, whatever. But the more you try to get to know them, the more you see that second fence, the one nearer to who they really are as a person. That fence is pretty high. They don't let just anybody in.

With Canadians, it's just the opposite. The outer fence is the high one. If you approach them too quickly with friendly small talk, they move away. Canadians are quieter with strangers. You don't see people walking down the street waving at everyone they pass. It's not a matter of them not being friendly. It's just that they don't think it's appropriate to be so forward to strangers.

We had to learn about that. It was important to not be too forward with people when we first met them. Give them time and let them watch you for a while. Because I am an introvert, Canada was, in a lot of ways, the perfect place for me. It is my nature to get to know someone slowly and then warm up to them. That's the way most Canadians are, too.

Randy

Moving to Canada is a bit of a shock for evangelicals from the Bible Belt. There is such a cool reserve about the people. A lot of people we met were skeptical, anti-evangelical, anti-Bible. If you asked where they went to church, you would hear about them being baptized as a child. Many people had some head knowledge about Christianity, but seemed to have little passion for God.

It was like that among some of the churches, too; even the evangelical ones. In Texas, you might start a ministry and then go tell people what you are doing and see if they want to get on board. Not in Canada. Instead, I went to the pastors and asked them to pray about us starting some Christian clubs on the college campuses. We wanted to get them behind us, not working against us. We wanted something that benefitted all the churches. We prayed with them for six months. Part of that was getting them to join us in prayer. Part of it was giving them time to get used to the idea of us doing work on the campuses.

I was also the preaching pastor at a little church that was just starting up. That little church only had between five and fifteen people attending. I didn't get a salary. The other pastor had an inheritance, so he was pretty well fixed. I, on the other hand, had to raise money, pray for God to take care of us, and write letters seeking support.

How were we living? Off the sale of our home in California. But we knew if we were truly called by God, He would take care of us. And, sure enough, people soon began to give. We were in Vancouver for three years. Through a miracle, we were even able to buy a house.

Mary Ann

When we first moved to Vancouver, my life pretty much revolved around keeping house, making meals, and getting us all to the little mission church Randy was pastoring, along with taking care of the kids. At that time, we were renting a house while we waited for the sale of our house back in California.

We had been there about three months when we were able to buy the house we really wanted to buy. We moved in and it was my dream house! We moved in December. The following June, I was diagnosed with hypoglycemia, a condition where your body needs lots of protein. I was feeling so weak. The doctor said I needed to eat five or six meals a day. When you are hypoglycemic, you need to eat all the time, but keep it very high protein, low in carbohydrates, and low in sugars.

I got off the phone with the doctor who was explaining all this and the first thing I said was, "Okay, Randy, go buy me some Diet Cokes." They didn't have Diet Dr. Pepper in Canada then. It was the first time I had a diet drink in my life. I loved full strength sodas. It took me about six months to transition to diet drinks.

Something else that happened was that we had only been in Vancouver about six months when we were asked by a group of Canadian Christians to consider moving to Toronto. Why move? We just got there. That request continued and eventually we did move to Toronto, but that was later. We were also applying to the Home Mission Board of our denomination for funding. If we were approved, the funding would start as full support, but gradually decrease to zero over five years. That gave you time to raise other funding or become self-supporting. However, when we turned in our paperwork to the Home Mission Board, it kept getting lost.

Randy

Toronto was asking us to come because by that time I had a doctorate. They needed someone with the right credentials who was able to work on college campuses with students. They promised to put in a word with the International Mission Board on our behalf. But the IMB had told us no in the past. There was also some possibility of support from the Home Mission Board, which said it was interested in a combination of student work and church planting. We applied to both organizations simultaneously and asked God to guide us. The Home Mission Board lost our application.

The International Mission Board jumped on our application and ran with it. We were put on the fast track to move to Toronto. We were accepted to be IMB missionaries, but the caveat with them was that you can't own property in the country where you are working. Therefore, we had to sell Mary Ann's dream home in Vancouver. That transaction resulted in a three quarter of a million dollar financial loss. Ouch. Like I said, serving God can be an adventure.

Mary Ann

In the past, there had been a concern from the IMB regarding Randy's arms. They hadn't been able to see past the medical clearance necessary for us to be IMB missionaries. Also, they wanted to know about all the expenses pertaining to Randy's arms and the costs of replacing them. We kept turning in what they wanted and this time, two weeks after we submitted the paperwork, they called us to say we needed to come in June for an interview.

Normally, it takes two years to wade through the paperwork and processes. We completed it in six weeks. Some of the things that helped us were the fact we already lived in Canada and had our residency established. We also already had our passports. Because of the way they do medicine up there, Randy had lifetime care for his arms through the Canadian healthcare system. We were already assimilated to the Canadian culture and had experience working with students there.

Randy's sister, Nancy, and her husband, Don, and their three children flew to Vancouver to keep our kids and we flew to Richmond, Virginia, for the meeting. At the interviews, the IMB attitude was, "Okay, if you want the job, you can start right away. You go on salary August 1. Move to Toronto as soon as you can." In six weeks we went from living in Vancouver and raising our own funding to living in Toronto and being full-time missionaries with the International Mission Board.

Randy

At that time, Henry Blackaby was writing *Experiencing God* and he would bring portions of it to meetings we would have. He would bring pictures of the little stick figures he had drawn that were later worked into illustrations for the book. I actually got to help proofread *Experiencing God* before it was published, which was huge.

After Henry had been in Vancouver a couple of years, the denomination we were part of asked him to move to Georgia in the United States to start the National Prayer Ministry. It was sad to lose him after moving all the way to Canada to work with him. But God was also moving us to Toronto.

Mary Ann and I have always been committed to serving where the need was big, not seeking the biggest salary or the biggest limelight, or the biggest church. Instead, we ask, "God, where are we needed most?" It turned out that was Toronto. Toronto is the New York City of Canada, with lots of immigrants from all over the world. There were, at that time, one hundred thousand Chinese, and about the same number of people from South America, along with Muslims, Hindus, and almost any other ethnic or religious group you could imagine.

Because of the ethnic diversity of Toronto, I saw it as a huge opportunity to do international work and be a bridge to the nations. At that time, in spite of how large the city was, existing churches were struggling to reach new people and grow. One of our goals was to start churches that would be attractive to university students and young families.

Chapter 19

THE SANCTUARY

Randy

Our first five years in Toronto was learning how people outside the " Bible Belt" of the United States look at us. We were adjusting to the culture and learning the needs. Also, we worked to coordinate with other evangelical denominations, not just Baptists. We had to grow and broaden our mindset of the world.

Canada is far more tradition-oriented than the United States. Canadians have a loyalty to England, a loyalty to the trusted and familiar. They came out of a relationship with a state church, so they tend to be most comfortable with a religion that is staid and formal. Their religion might best be identified as large buildings, stained glass windows, and certified, very traditional clergy. What was lacking was a personal relationship with Jesus Christ.

In those days, evangelicals only made up two percent of the population in Canada. There was a real tension regarding whether people starting new evangelical churches could be perceived as "ordained enough," and "serious enough" to be considered legitimate.

Unfortunately, with all the big churches, highly educated clergy, and beautiful stained-glass windows that gave people such comfort, most of their traditional churches were in decline.

The stained glass doesn't bring people in. But Canadians at that time were leery of churches without all the stained glass. When Canadians see an evangelical church, they want to know if it's "real" Christianity. And if so, they then ask themselves do they even want real Christianity?

You see this sentiment a lot: "My grandparents went to church and they were bored, but they went anyway. My parents went to church and they were bored, so they quit going. Why should I want to go? It's boring." But churches that aren't boring are perceived as cults or at least borderline cults. There is always that tension.

Through the 1980s, Canadian churches that came from the Baptist tradition were almost all started by people from small towns in the southern United States. Those individuals believed church was the center of life. They went from being a highly respected person in their hometown to being seen as an invader and possible cult member when they moved to Canada. That was quite a shock for a lot of them.

When you move from the United States to Canada, you don't want to give up your identity. On the other hand, how do you come across as relevant in a culture where religion is perceived by almost everyone in the ways I described? This is something for anyone trying to make a difference to consider when they move into a new environment: How do you escape the centripetal force of your background? How do you move toward the cutting edge? How do you find new ways to share a Gospel that never changes? People who can't answer those questions successfully are going to face a lot of frustration.

Before I sound too radical, let me say that Christ never changes. God is the same yesterday, today, and forever. But the ways we interface with our fellow man do change. Is it through the work you do, through social services, through door-to-door inviting of people, through neighborhood Bible studies? For most people, church is a meeting held at 11 a.m. on Sunday morning. After you have done that, you are through for the week. It's an obligation, not a relationship.

In many places, church must look different than that 11 o'clock stereotype or you have lost people before they even give you a try. It needs to be family-based, home-based, and highly relevant. We saw that as we tried to work through the existing small churches in Vancouver and Toronto. What the missionaries accepted as the "legitimate model of church" limited many of them from ever reaching people or being effective.

Many of the missionaries thought it was disloyal to tradition to try anything new. So we decided, along with another missionary couple, Barry and LaWanda Bonney, to get involved in some creative church planting. Barry was the church planter, and I was the student worker. We realized for a church to really reach people, it needed to be exciting, and not bound by tradition. It had to be creative. It needed to relate to professionals who didn't usually go to church and weren't usually coming from a church background.

We also needed to appeal to students. What I wanted was to start a church for college students, but that wasn't permitted. We were told by the organizational leaders it was our job to get the students to whom we ministered to attend the local churches. But the students just couldn't relate to those churches. The churches were small and trapped in the past.

Every Friday morning we met with the Bonneys for prayer. Every Friday afternoon the four of us would drive around the various communities praying. We asked God to give us a church to reach the people in these neighborhoods, along with university students. Where should we start the new church? How do we start? Who should lead it? Who would come?

After much prayer, the four of us decided to start a fund to raise money for this as yet non-existent church. We pooled our tithes for two years and used that money as seed funds to help start the congregation. We even wrote a constitution, value statements, everything for the church, though it didn't even exist yet. God had put this non-existent church on our hearts. It was a "vision" we would see become a reality.

So you had these two poor missionary families trying to save their tithes to start something radical in an environment where all the powers that be, whether they were Baptist or Church of England, said it was the last thing they wanted. To give you an example of these existing churches, one had seventeen members and another had twenty-nine. Of those, all but four were mentally or physically disabled. Those churches were ministering to the needs of those seventeen and twenty-nine people, sure. But what about the masses on whom they were having no effect at all? And what was there in those congregations that would make other people want to start going there? If they were going to be effective, it would have already happened. But it didn't happen. There needed to be something else going on, an alternative.

We did have one friendship going with a large downtown church near the university. It would have been an ideal place to build a student ministry. Their pastor said we could partner together for three to five years and build a student ministry using their building, which was largely empty. The pastor said, "When you are ready to take these students and start a new church, we will support you and help you do that."

However, the old traditionalists – well-meaning but misguided – called a stop to the student ministry. I mean they shut it all down. They didn't want us to work with any other groups or people from the outside. If they couldn't reach young people with methods that were fifty or a hundred years old, then they were satisfied not reaching them.

Once again, people have trouble understanding that the truths of the Gospel are unchanging, but the ways people relate to one another change all the time. The "right way to reach people" is a moving target. Therefore, worship styles and outreach styles have to be flexible. To be effective, you must be willing to change.

Can you imagine a church that said, "We aren't going to have telephones, because there weren't telephones when this church began?" Or, "No the ministers can't have cell phones" because there weren't cell phones fifty years ago? But churches decide all the time to reject ministry styles because they are new or different.

So we lost the opportunity for a wonderful, cooperative ministry. The bottom line was that there wasn't one single healthy, dynamic, growing church in our network of churches that would appeal to the college students with whom I was working. That was going to be the focus of this new church we were planning and praying for: young professionals with families and college students.

So Barry and I decided we needed to pool our tithes and see if we could find a creative pastor, and someone who could lead music. We would also have to find the rest of the people necessary to put together a ministry team. At that time, there were some short-term mission teams coming from the United States to help us. We had them do experimental Backyard Bible Clubs in some of the neighborhoods. Backyard Bible Clubs are similar to a Vacation Bible School, but they are held in neighborhoods, instead of at a church. Those teams also did some canvasing of a neighborhood where we thought there was the greatest possibility of starting a successful work.

Canvasing involved finding out what residents perceived to be the needs within that community. When you're doing community development, in order to put programs in place that can make a real difference in people's lives, you first need to discover what the real needs are. I've learned it's a mistake to just go in and say, "Here's what we've got to offer." In a very friendly way, we went through the neighborhoods talking to people who'd give us a few minutes. We'd ask them, "If you could solve one problem in this community, what would it be? What are the needs of which you're aware?"

They'd tell us about the things that were discouraging or limiting families. We let them talk. From the list of all those needs, we asked ourselves, "Which of these needs could our group meet? What resources or techniques do we have that we could mobilize? We can't do everything, but is there one thing we can do to really help?" We looked at the community needs and our abilities, talents, and resources, and tried to find an intersection of the two.

It was the community of Oakville, Ontario, located southwest of Toronto along Lake Ontario. It was an upscale, growing area near a college where I had a successful ministry going. There was very little church participation. It was a suburb where executives were moving. In their move, they were leaving far behind any church they had ever attended.

We looked around this area and prayed over it for two years. Barry had a friend, a really dynamic guy named Jeff Christopherson. He had previously wanted to start a church in that area. However, the area coordinator kept telling him no. So instead, Jeff put together a team and started a very successful church in Calgary, in the western part of Canada.

Barry and Jeff were friends, so Barry sent him a note asking if he would assist us in finding someone to help start the church. Well, Jeff is actually the one who responded. He planned a trip to Toronto to meet with us. He said he had someone who was interested in leading music. He wanted to know if he could bring the guy along to explore possibilities. We said, "Sure, but there has to be an understanding you're both coming on faith. Other than our two families' tithes, there is no budget."

A few days later, Barry told us Jeff had a couple from Florida, Jim and Joy Danielson, who were praying about being part of the team. Joy was a registered nurse. If she could get a work visa, at least one of them would have some income. From the saved tithe money we had enough cash for plane tickets, which we donated to bring everyone together. When everyone arrived, we gathered the families in one little house. They really got to know each other. The atmosphere was charged with excitement. Everyone could sense God's presence. We felt his approval and guidance. We prayed and prayed and then started planning. It was my privilege to preach the first sermon, which was from Isaiah 61 on being oaks of righteousness before the Lord, an appropriate topic since we were in Oakville.

After that, everyone went back to their homes, whether that was in Calgary or Florida. They started raising funds. We also started spreading the word that we believed God was about to do something big in Oakville. People were resigning their jobs and moving to Oakville to be a part of what was happening.

Others were going on "fishing expeditions" in some of the neighborhoods. They would meet families and start home Bible studies. We also held events in parks and invited families from the surrounding neighborhoods. We wanted them to see we cared about their kids; we weren't a cult; and we offered something worthwhile, free, and family-oriented.

Something interesting happened, however. One of the things we learned is that if we were having an event for the kids, people wouldn't come unless we charged. They thought that if it was free, there must be strings attached. If we charged, they didn't feel obligated to come back if they didn't like the program. That's what I mean about being willing to convey old truths in a new way. It might be offensive to someone from the Bible Belt to think of charging to come to an event that would be free in Texas or Georgia. But in the Toronto area, people felt more comfortable being charged rather than attending a free event. We were willing to adapt.

When we did surveys, there was great interest in solid moral training for children. We thought of that as a niche we could meet. Christianity has the best moral system in the world. Let's share it, and at the same time, share Jesus. When parents brought their children, they found the events were well-organized. They also saw that the people hosting the events were educated professionals. The parents who brought their children and the people working on our team were individuals who could look each other in the eye and find common ground.

The Canadians wanted to find people hosting these open-air events who made them feel comfortable. When that happened, it gave us credibility. These were people who had left, or never attended, church. However, they still wanted moral training for their children. We were creating safe places to think about spiritual things and ask questions. That was a big deal. We were building relationships and having conversations. Another thing that was different about this new church was that there wasn't a timeline on when things had to happen. Everything was God's timing. We had a vision of what could be. We offered outreach Bible studies, discussion groups, home fellowships, and children's activities.

From there, we gathered interested people and had occasional worship services to demonstrate what it would be like if we did have a church. They were called Preview Services. The services featured upbeat music, creative sermons, and an emphasis on meeting needs rather than preaching dogma and theology. When we had the launch service, it was extremely exciting. The church would be called The Sanctuary. We were able to rent a public school to use. Another denomination had a house they let us rent, which became our operations center.

Those of us working in Toronto were like a family of church planters instead of one couple out on their own. That was also a new way of doing things. Everyone shared ideas, came together to meet, and prayed. No one was alone. If anyone had a project they needed help with, others could step in and assist. If someone was struggling, they were refreshed by the rest of the team. It was the way the first churches were started in the New Testament. The Sanctuary now has two campuses in Oakville and one each in Burlington, Brampton, Mississauga, Kerr Village, Pickering, and North York.

Keep in mind, I was sent to the area to work with college students. So how does that work tie in with what was happening at The Sanctuary? The first adult baptized at the church was a college student who came to Christ through the ministry in Oakville. Then other students started coming. The church really started to grow based on young families, but college students felt very comfortable there. They didn't have to check their intellect at the door.

What did it take for this incredible work to happen in an area that is reported to have the lowest per capita church attendance in North America? The people who came to help start The Sanctuary were risk takers, visionaries, people willing to try new ways of doing things. They were willing to meet needs in non-traditional ways. Anyone who has been involved in a traditional church and wants to try a new way to do things knows that tradition is a hard chain to break. There is certainly a place for tradition, but in a lot of situations, it simply makes people feel so comfortable they no longer feel challenged, no longer grow. And after a while, they stop coming. They feel like, "Oh, yeah, Christianity. I have that all figured out."

As I said, the centripetal force of tradition can be hard to break away from. Of course, all the core essentials were kept: baptism, worship, prayer, and communion. We were looking for a strategy that worked, but the truths are eternal and unchanging. Doing research for my doctorate, one of the greatest things I learned was Jesus' approach for training people. It was through the power of modeling, the power of example. Jesus was a revolutionary. It was the traditionalists of His day who put Him to death. They valued tradition over truth. It has been said that having models to follow is essential. We all live based on the modeling we have seen in others. We can follow the model of the revolutionary Jesus or we can follow tradition.

There are three words in the Greek New Testament for this modeling. My favorite is *hupogrammos*. That's a word picture for how to perfectly form the letters of the alphabet. Remember how in elementary school there was a perfect alphabet above the blackboard? You were supposed to learn from the perfect letters and practice writing them yourself underneath. If you couldn't remember how to make a letter you could always look up at the perfect letters. Following Christ is like that. He set the perfect model – the example. We learn the basic "life" alphabet of Jesus. From that alphabet we can make our own words and write the book of our lives. We get our vocabulary of life from Jesus. He modeled love, forgiveness, sacrifice, and compassion; everything we need. When we use Jesus as our *hupogrammos*, the one who gives us our alphabet of life, we become a living Bible for others.

Looking back, most of the churches that had been started in Canada up to that time – and probably in most places – were modeled on the churches where those people came from. We realized that in the Toronto area we needed new models. Some might ask how we kept the message of Jesus from getting watered down while breaking with tradition and creating safe places for lots of unsaved people to ask spiritual questions. In some churches, people feel safe because anything goes. They believe there are no absolute truths, so they can believe whatever they want.

That's certainly not what we were about. We were safe because we placed a high value on people. The theology was never compromised and the teachings were straight from the Bible. It was about, and is about, God and man, love and forgiveness. We were also convinced if we rushed people along their spiritual journey or pressured them to make a decision, we would drive them away. At the same time, the people of the Toronto area realized, "Hey, these people do good work, care about us, give wise counsel, have a relationship with Jesus Christ that's authentic, and are genuinely compassionate. And they aren't trying to get our money."

It was also clear to us that people watch you. They watch to see if you're legitimate. Can you be trusted? We first moved to Toronto in January in the midst of a snowstorm. In the spring, when the ice was melting and Mary Ann was walking our kids to school, a lady walked up to her and asked how she was doing. The lady said she knew we were from somewhere else.

She told Mary Ann, "We have been watching you for three months and wanted to come and say hello." That's just the Canadian way. We made all these great friendships up and down the block by serving their families and caring about them. But we had to go slow. If we had gotten in a hurry, it might have made them defensive; it might have pushed people away.

Another lady that Mary Ann met at a children's soccer game began asking questions about Christianity. Over time, her faith began to grow. Now she works for a Christian ministry in Canada. She came to know Christ at a deeper level as a result of conversations that started at that soccer game. That illustrates the importance of building relationships, not just trying to transplant evangelical traditions from one part of the world to another.

Chapter 20

WE INTERRUPT THIS PROGRAM

Randy

    I used to believe God gave us a task and we went out and did it. We were rewarded if we did it and missed out on the reward if we didn't. It wasn't so much about a relationship or listening to the Lord's voice. God gave us a job, we went out and did it, and then reported back. But it was all about us doing it and Him blessing it.

    Now I see things very differently. Learning to live the Christian life is a lot like learning to play the piano. First you learn the basics. You learn the keys and how to play scales. The better you learn the basics, the freer you are to play any song that comes into your heart. The more you know the basics of the Christian faith, the more the great teacher, Jesus, can guide and direct you every day.

    An important technique in growing as a Christian is learning key, foundational truths from the Bible. My BSU director, Rollin Delap, taught me years ago that the key concepts in the Bible are the foundational principles for establishing boundaries and living successfully. Knowing the Bible helps protect you from destructive choices.

    Some of the key statements I memorized in the Bible were promises from God to believers about things He will do for us in response to faith and obedience. I experimented with this and saw it become reality in my life. It's not about legalism or having to do this by such-and-such time. In fact, it's just the opposite.

The more I know about Jesus through the Bible and prayer, the more I know how to live a successful life. I didn't learn the Bible to get God to like me. I did it to learn the thoughts of God and His promises for His followers. It's one of the most productive things a person can do.

Previously, I saw Christians as being sent out *by* Jesus. Now I see it as a journey *with* Jesus. Most Christians have a mental list of things they must do and must not do. The do's and don'ts are just boundaries. Far more importantly, Jesus Christ is calling us into a friendship with Him. In a friendship, it's not about the rules, it's about the relationship. In relationships, both people talk and both people listen.

People often say, "I don't hear God speaking to me." The question is this: How can we hear God speaking if we won't be still to listen? Part of the journey is learning to listen. That was part of the beauty of the team that came together for The Sanctuary. It was a team of people dedicated to the journey and to listening to God.

Mary Ann

In the year 2000, we could see all these things coming together in Toronto with The Sanctuary. But part of our journey was about to take us out of Canada and back to Lubbock, Texas. On the Friday before spring break, my aunt called and said, "Mary Ann, you need to get down here and decide what you're going to do with your parents."

She told me, "Your dad is in the hospital and he says he can't take care of your mother anymore by himself. I'll stay here until you get here, but you need to come take care of your parents."

178

I had been going back to Lubbock to see them once or twice a year, but I had no idea anything was wrong. My parents were keeping it from me. I knew they had stopped traveling two years earlier, but I didn't realize things had gone downhill so fast.

My brother Mike, who had been one of the original hippies and gone to Fort Worth to start a flower business, had been living with my parents for the last year and a half. That's because he was living with injuries caused by being shot six times during a robbery in Fort Worth.

In 1992, Mike had a small window washing business. He was working one night at a convenience store washing the windows. There was a clerk at the store who was working to support her five children. It was just the clerk and my brother in there. At 9:30 pm, three seventeen-year-olds walked in to rob the place. They shot the clerk once and severed her spine. They shot Mike six times and left him for dead. He crawled across the store to a phone and called 911. He was in the hospital three months the first time around. There were many hospitalizations after that, too. He lost most of his digestive system. That made it difficult for him to eat.

He never knew if food was going to stay down. He had nausea and vomiting and diarrhea, often up to thirty times a day. He was six-foot-four-inches tall and one hundred and sixty-four pounds when he was shot. When he died, March 11, 1999, he weighed ninety-eight pounds. He lived that last year with my parents in Lubbock. Before he died, he told me that Mom was getting forgetful. I would respond, "She is just getting older."

He would come back with, "But she's also being mean." She had never been a forgetful person or mean. Mike wasn't the easiest person to be around. He told me Mom was supposed to bring him something and would go to get it and never come back. At the time, I didn't think too much about it. My brother was kind of a complainer, so I just thought he was complaining. There also just wasn't as much information about Alzheimer's then. Now, when people start talking about forgetfulness, everyone think's Alzheimer's. That wasn't so true back then. Looking back now, I know it was the beginning of Alzheimer's. The only real clue I had at the time was when my mom was writing a letter to someone. She asked me, "How do you spell LOOK?"

When we came back to live in Lubbock, Mom was about seventy-eight and my dad was eighty-three. He was in the hospital and he was telling me, "Your mom keeps saying she's going to do the taxes, but Mary Ann, she can't do it."

He told me she was forgetting stuff. Taking care of her had simply exhausted him. She was doing things like trying to take her medicines twice when they were only to be taken once. My parents would get in a big fuss because he would try to stop her from taking them twice in a row, and she couldn't remember taking them. That kind of thing, taking two doses instead of one, can be really dangerous.

However, she still appeared to be functional and wanted to go places and make decisions on her own. Sometimes she was fine and sometimes not. It was hard to anticipate which was which. My foster sister Sherry had moved to Germany previously, but was moving back to Kansas. She came down, and we talked about what to do. Sherry needed to make a certain amount of money each month. We worked out an agreement so she could stay with my parents and help them alternating every two weeks with me until June when my kids got out of school. In July, we moved back to Lubbock from our home in Canada. We had a year of work we could do in the United States while still being employed by the International Mission Board. We could also take up to two years leave of absence, so that's what we did.

During that time, we realized my parents were not getting any better and we would have to resign and not return to Toronto. We resigned in the summer of 2003. I didn't really struggle with the move, because I had told Randy years before we ever married, that my brother wouldn't really be in a position to take care of them. We knew all along that someday we were going to need to take care of my parents.

Randy

My mom had worked up to age seventy-two. She had some digestive problems, a pinched nerve in her leg, and scoliosis in her back. So, at seventy-two, she retired from her job working for the Federal Aviation Administration. Her health went downhill really fast. She had also been a heavy smoker for forty years with no exercise.

In her fifties, she had been diagnosed with cancer. Surgery and radiation had cured her, but the powerful treatments eventually damaged her small intestines. She had a hard time eating and swallowing. She was hospitalized to remove some of her small intestine. She almost died then, but they brought her back. It took her months to recuperate. Later she started having congestive heart failure.

I flew down from Canada and was with her for a week. She went into the hospital and then to a transition hospital for some therapy. I went back to Toronto because we thought she was getting better. In the spring of 1999, during an especially busy time in my university work with students and while preparing for The Sanctuary, I got a call that Mom was getting worse.

A week later Mom had a heart attack and died. I was so close to my mom, even though at that time there were a lot of miles between us. She had always been this encouraging, loving person and we had a deep mother/son connection. She never tried to hold me back or tell me I couldn't do something because of my arms. She wanted me to get married and have the life I wanted.

Unfortunately, she was never as close to the Lord after my accident. She was a Christian and had Christian beliefs, but I don't think she was able to work through what happened. She had only been actively involved in church for a few years. She also got her feelings hurt at the church she attended. Things like that happen. Somebody says something. Somebody else gets their feelings hurt and blames the entire church and quits being involved. They let a bad experience with one person become a wedge between them and God.

I think Mom also had a certain resentment of God for letting this accident happen. She felt betrayed by God. She allowed roots of bitterness to take hold in her heart. When that happens, it is very difficult for anyone to reach you. Outwardly, she was the kindest person. Inwardly, she struggled to forgive those involved in my accident. She struggled to forgive God for allowing it to happen.

My brother, Rex, also had an accident some years after mine. He was an inventor with a brilliant mind, just like my dad. With only one semester of college, he became a millionaire twice over. How? He worked as an inventor for a start-up company in the developing mobile telecommunications industry.

However, he was an extreme risk taker. He kept pushing the envelope with extreme sports like parasailing and hang gliding. He had a serious accident and shattered one leg. His company told him to stay away from dangerous activities. His hobbies were too big a risk and the company needed him. However, he was an adrenaline junkie and the temptation was too much for him. If he couldn't do the sports, he at least wanted to be right there to watch friends participating in them.

One day, in January of 1992, he was at the edge of a mountain with a bunch of people who were hang gliding. The wind kicked up and he got tangled in the cords of a person's hang glider. When the glider took off, Rex was thrown off the mountain. He tumbled down, breaking bones all along the way. When he finally came to a stop, he was alert and awake. He was rescued and transferred to a hospital nearby. Tragically, in surgery, he had a blood clot or a blockage which stopped the flow of blood to the motor section of his brain. Essentially, it was a massive stroke. He was left completely paralyzed from right below his eyes to his toes.

His accident happened in California. Mom flew from Fort Worth and I flew from Canada. Doctors believed he wouldn't live. If he did, they said he would only be able to communicate through eye blinks. When it appeared he would die, I went to a solitary place and prayed to God like I never had before. Basically, I asked that God would spare Rex's life. God honored that prayer. However, Rex is still paralyzed to this day. Looking back, I wish I had left the matter entirely in God's hands and said, "Thy will be done." Only God knew the future for my brother and what was best for him.

Only Rex could say whether he's glad to have lived all these years, or would have rather been in heaven all this time. By Rex's choice, we don't communicate much, but I still pray for him often. There are some heart-breaks in life you can't fix, no matter how much you try.

Obviously, his accident was hard on my Mom, too. A week before she died, I had a long conversation and prayer with her. She reconfirmed her faith in God, and prayed for His help and His peace. When she died, she was finally freed from her heartbreaks. Her death was far more emotional for me than my father's passing, simply because my mother and I had been so much closer.

Then, about one year after my mother's death, Mary Ann got the call from her aunt about her parents. Looking back, we can see her mom was hiding the onset of Alzheimer's. We would talk to her on the phone and there would be areas where instead of being specific about certain things, she would just be very vague.

Mary Ann suggested we go to Lubbock for a month, but I could tell this wasn't going to be just a month-long issue. We decided to move back to Lubbock and take care of them. We got her parents into an assisted-living situation. That worked for a year until her Dad needed help at night with her Mom.

There was a house next door to the one we were living in that was for sale. The house payment was a quarter of what the monthly assisted-living bill was. If we moved them next door to us, they could eat meals with us and it would be easier for us to check on them at any time of day or night. A simple baby monitor allowed us to keep track of things from next door. If they called out, we could come running.

Later, as they got worse, we did have to hire some people to come help us. It became clear, by the end of that first year, that we weren't going back to Canada any time soon. It also meant we were no longer collecting a salary and we lost all our medical benefits.

Needless to say, this was another period of extreme faith. I was praying, "God, what can I do here in Lubbock to both support my family and stay in missions?" Let me point out, though, that we never considered what was going on with Mary Ann's parents as something that prevented us from following the will of God. God's will for our lives never contradicts scripture. And scripture is very clear to honor your father and mother.

Her parents had helped us all our married lives. We both knew we needed to move back to Texas and take care of them. Just the same, as a longtime BSU director doing missions and campus outreach, I was a fish out of water when we moved back to Lubbock. I had grown used to being a missionary to an un-churched area. Now we were moving back to West Texas, where there are hundreds of churches, large and small, to choose from. I used to say if you were traveling through Lubbock and fell asleep while driving, there was a pretty good chance you would hit a church.

Coming back to Texas showed me something really important. Only about twenty-five percent of the people, even in the Bible Belt, were attending all those churches. I realized that Lubbock was a mission field, too. Most people in West Texas know enough about Christianity to have a conversation with you and tell you how they were baptized as a child or went to this or that Vacation Bible School. No matter what you ask them, it's "Oh yeah, I've been there" or "I've done that."

There is a real spirit of religiosity, which, like tradition, is another counterfeit for a real relationship with Jesus. I hear things like, "My uncle is a preacher, so I know all about that Christianity stuff." Or they will tell you about the church they attend at Christmas and Easter but no other time. They do it to keep you at arm's length. That way you don't find out they're spiri-tually empty.

Churches in Lubbock were adding a few here and there to their numbers, but not really multiplying. There is a difference between holding classes on religion and actually reaching out to people and making disciples. I had the opportunity to begin teaching dis-cipleship at one of these churches. I went from doing mission out-reach in the Toronto area to doing it in Lubbock.

But I still missed the opportunity to start something new, to be a part of something really growing. My nature is to start new things. If I was still an engineer, I'd definitely be an inventor. I am more the church planter type than the type of person who enjoys holding down a position at the same place for a long period of time.

Mary Ann

We knew it wasn't practical for my parents to come live with us in Canada. This was a window of time for us to go back to Texas and take care of them. When we first came down, we tried a senior assisted living facility. They served three meals a day and had apartments they could live in and lots of activities. They liked the dinner rolls at that place a lot. It was fine for a little over a year. But in 2001, Dad said, "Your mom is getting up and wandering around so much at night I can't get any sleep. I need someone here to watch your mother."

For five years, after buying the house next door, we took care of them. We went from paying $2,400 a month for caregivers to help my dad and the cost of the assisted living facility to $700 a month for a house payment on the house next door. We also cut a gate in the fence so we could combine backyards.

I can still vividly remember the first time my mom didn't recognize me. She introduced me to someone as her sister. I said, "No, I am her daughter Mary Ann." She said, "Oh, that's right; my daughter." That's hard. Very hard. Another change in her was that she went from being this very kind woman who accepted everyone to something else. We were sitting in the doctor's office one day. She looked at this woman and said, "She is just too fat!" She said it really loud, too.

The hard part, among other things, was that when you looked at her, she seemed perfectly normal. But for those of us who knew her, we could tell something was really wrong. Keep in mind that my mother had always been a person who valued self-control. She would sometimes come home and tell us about something that happened at work. I would say, "Aren't you mad? Aren't you going to tell them off?"

She would respond, "Oh no, because that won't accomplish anything. It would just cause more hurt in this situation, and I'm not going to do that." If people did mean things to her, she had a huge capacity to forgive.

So, when she blurted out how fat the person was, I wanted to crawl under the floor and die. Something like that would never have come out of my mother's mouth when she was in control of her faculties. I grieved over that. Also, by the time I was in Lubbock again, she was so far gone I never got to have a real heart-to-heart conversation with her. I so wanted to just ask her for every single pearl of wisdom she had to offer.

Even though she was up and moving around, the person she had been all her life, the dynamic leader, was gone. However, a few pieces of that person remained –the gracious, kind, polite person was still there ninety-nine percent of the time. On a few occasions, Mother became difficult to handle. The first time it happened, it was due to the doctor changing her medicine. The medicine she was on kept her calmed down, but it caused a shuffling of the feet. When the medicine was changed, she could walk better, but she was more agitated. We learned to adjust the dose so she could walk better without so much agitation.

Another difficult thing was watching my dad grieve as she slipped away. He was losing the wife to whom he gave his heart. Mom was bedfast for the last nine months of her life. By this time, I had really gone through all the stages of grieving and could see we weren't going to get her back.

In March of 2004, I went down to Kerrville, Texas, to visit our former BSU director, Mike Lundy, and his wife, who was a clinical psychologist. I said, "Jan, I need to talk to you." They had taken care of her mother-in-law for years in their home and then needed the help of a medical facility. I asked Jan, "How will I know when it's time? How will I know when it's simply impossible for us to take care of my mom at home?"

Jan said, "You will know. You will just know." I needed a respite and going down there to see them did me a world of good. I was also reminded that the Lord will never give us more than we can bear. I came back and said, "Okay Lord, please tell me when I need to put my mother in a facility because I am exhausted and I don't know how much more I can take." That was in March. In April, God took my mother home. Her Alzheimer's was healed.

Mom died April 13, 2004. I had the opportunity to speak at her funeral. At that time I said, "People ask me, 'Why didn't you put your mother in a home. She didn't remember you anymore.' But those people had it backwards. She forgot who I was, but I never forgot who she was."

Dad lived for another fifteen months. He did pretty well for most of the next year. Then he got a bedsore on his heel. That meant he had to use a wheelchair. Because he wasn't walking, he got weaker. Finally, we had to get him a hospital bed and he had another medical flare up from an infection. He was hospitalized and then had to be at a long-term care hospital for three months. During his time there, I asked him, "If you could do anything before you die what would it be?"

You know what he said? "I want to lead one more person to the Lord."

Any time someone came in the room, he would ask them, "Do you know how much Jesus loves you?" He would remind them to take their troubles to the Lord. He kept his Bible and Sunday school lesson book beside him at all times. And he lived out the words on those pages. He cared about people. He wanted people to know that Jesus loved them. The day before he died, we were visiting him. He said, "In my quiet time this morning, Jesus told me I'm going home today."

We asked if he needed a doctor. He told us that it was all okay. We told him the doctor was coming in the morning at nine. At 8:15 the next morning, Dad died in his sleep. It was exactly how I had prayed he would go, peacefully in his sleep.

To show you what kind of heart my dad had, back before my mom died, he called and said, "Mary Ann, if there is any money left after we are both gone, I want you to buy something that you would like to have, but would normally never buy for yourself. That will be your mother's and my last present to you." A year or two after he died, I had rotator cuff surgery. I had been confined to the house for ten days and was getting antsy. There was a new car show at the Lubbock Civic Center, so I asked Randy if he wanted to go for an hour or two.

We were walking around and saw the Toyota Avalon for the first time. It had a push button starter. That was pretty cool. It had all kinds of push-button stuff. I thought that was really neat because, although Randy loves to drive, manipulating keys is the bane of his existence. Keys require a lot of dexterity.

That day I said to myself, "I don't know when, but I think that's what we are going to buy with the money." We had been married thirty-something years and had never once bought a new car. Randy could always find one that was two or three years old and not pay all that extra money to drive a new one off the lot. But this time we bought a new one; a Toyota Avalon with a push button starter. Thanks, Mom and Dad! It is a really great gift.

Chapter 21

ADVENTURES IN ASIA

Randy

In the middle of 2001, I had the opportunity to go on a mission trip to Asia. It reawakened my call for reaching the nations. This is while we were taking care of Mary Ann's parents. By the end of that year, my furlough was running out and I accepted a full-time position with a mission group working in that part of the world. I was literally working for the International Mission Board one day and this other organization the next, without missing a beat. I became their development officer. It was a natural transition, even though I'd never been a development officer before. My responsibilities were to promote projects in Asia, seek financial support, and find volunteers to join us.

However, when 9/11 happened and the United States was attacked, giving to many missions projects fell off a cliff. The stock market went way down, as well, which hurt people's finances and investment earnings. People were afraid of foreign countries. It was hunker-down time.

People were giving to 9/11 survivors and not much else. There was also this clash-of-civilizations mentality of "they are coming to attack us, so why should we help them?" Because of the drop in giving, my salary was cut back, and then cut back again. I had to find another avenue of support. I was fortunate enough to become a part-time missions' pastor at Indiana Avenue Baptist Church. Therefore, we could funnel as much money as possible to the workers in Asia because they didn't have another source of income.

At Indiana Avenue, I worked as a part-time teacher, "disciple-trainer," and speaker. An old friend, Russ Murphy, and a wonderful pastor named Jim Gerlt helped open that door. That led to doing outreach Bible studies, working with the poor, and using my pastoral care abilities. I led them to start several new outreach programs. Those programs are still going on at that church, even though I'm not currently a part of them. We trained laymen and they carried on and expanded those programs.

Fortunately, in the years after 9/11, giving has taken an upswing for our work in Asia. We are doing a great deal of outreach there in different capacities. After the Great Sichuan Earthquake of 2008, we began working with educators to help the people. That earthquake left more than eighty-seven thousand people dead or missing. Four million others had to flee from their homes. Many are still unaccounted for and presumed dead. Even after all this time, reclamation work is still going on.

The quake struck on the afternoon of May 12, 2008. Schools were still in session, businesses were open, homes collapsed, and many elderly and little children were among those killed. The mountains and areas surrounding Chengdu suffered a lot of damage. You had whole villages cut off and the Chinese government had to send one hundred thousand soldiers to try to dig them out.

For the first time in modern history, China was willing to accept relief from outside countries and agencies. The magnitude of the disaster opened doors. We have someone in our group who speaks Cantonese, Mandarin, English, Spanish, and numerous Chinese mountain dialects. Because he was nearby, he was able to get there quickly. He became a networker for aid groups from Canada and the United States, as well as other countries.

We also had relationships with some educators there. We provided grief counseling for those who lost loved ones. In the Chinese legal system, each family is allowed only one child. Because so many schools were in session and the damage was so extensive, many of those children were killed.

Therefore, those families lost their only child. In the Chinese economy and family structure, that one child is counted on to get a good enough job to support his parents in their old age. He or she also has to support the grandparents if they are still living. You could think of it as an upside down pyramid of people which that child is expected to support. In other words, that child is the retirement income for his or her parents. Losing one child means losing your support system. A person of thirty could be supporting his parents, his wife's parents, and any living grandparents. Maybe as many as eight people are in the background that just lost their future support when that child died in the earthquake. The grief over losing a child in China is really beyond imagination.

In the midst of that earthquake, we had been propelled from small projects into a new level of working with international relief organizations. We trained Chinese school teachers from the earthquake area to look for suicide warning signs and depression in students, the parents, and other teachers.

We began by training sixty school teachers from thirty different major school districts affected by the quake. We were teaching them to be the grief counseling trainers among their faculty and staff. We were able to get ten thousand sets of counseling books – a total of sixty-thousand books – printed and distributed in the public schools. The multiplication of trained grief counselors, combined with the interactive grief counseling books designed for children, helped prevent suicides and gave people hope.

Now, we are able to present the curriculum to education bureaus from three hundred areas across China. In just two and a half years, God has catapulted one Chinese national who was willing to serve, along with me and a few others, from a small ministry to a group that is working with many relief agencies and educational institutions across China.

We believe this can change the lives of tens of thousands of kids. Through that, God has helped us focus on the next generation of Chinese. That country has four hundred million young people under the age of twenty-nine. They are looking for purpose in life. They are asking if there is anything more to life than good grades, a job, a car, and an apartment. Is success the answer?

Many parents are pressuring them to perform to the point of driving them to suicide. Teachers are also putting enormous pressure on them. But a few of the schools are realizing that this is having some very negative effects. We also see that many of the teachers are under so much pressure they are killing themselves.

The teachers that survived the earthquake were, out of desperation, put in military rescue vehicles with as many as fifty or sixty children and told, "You are now their parent." Some of them didn't get to bury their own spouse or child. They just had to get in the truck and go. Some teachers were committing suicide out of grief and anxiety.

To their credit, I think the authorities and the army did an incredible job digging out the people they could find. They also had the horrible task of disposing of thousands upon thousands of dead bodies to stop the spread of diseases. Frankly, I'm concerned regarding what the effects will be down the line for those eighteen- and twenty-year-old soldiers. How will they handle all the traumatic things they have been through? Will they have post-traumatic stress disorder in their future?

Through this disaster, and because God placed one of our people near where it happened, we have had a voice in the Chinese education system as it deals with this. One of the professors we have been working with since the earthquake has such a heart for the people. She has led her university to create a hybrid program linking social work and psychology. There is also an emphasis on reaching students with a message of hope.

We are helping form the curriculum and the teaching. We are also helping create a field service program for the university. They have forty-five thousand students on one campus and twenty-five thousand on another. We are also bringing teachers who know values, curriculum, and counseling to lead conferences for the teachers. We are working with teachers, parents, and troubled youth.

Our Chinese friends keep asking us to enlarge the program. The only thing holding us back is the funding to move forward. We have plenty of volunteers and once we have the funding, we can expand. Sichuan is an influential province, and the work we do there will have an effect on all of China.

For example, we have been invited to present curriculum to educators from three hundred school districts across China. One of our representatives was able to stand up and say, "Our curriculum is one of faith, hope, and love. Here's why every Chinese child needs faith...Here's why every Chinese child needs hope...Here's why every Chinese child needs love...and here is how we teach it." He was swarmed with requests to come and do more presentations.

Our philosophy is to go as servants to those who influence Chinese education. We see a need and we try to serve the people and meet that need. Jesus said of himself in Mark 10:45, "For even the Son of Man came not to be served, but to serve..." We are following Jesus's example. God is honoring that plan because it came from Him. The needs are many. For example, we see the dramatic need for values curriculum in China. From birth, children have been taught there is no God. Their parents and their grandparents were told there is no God. If you have no God, no standard, no revelation, then who do you obey? The one with the biggest stick?

The government is striving to achieve a "harmonious society," but that's a difficult task. They have one point three billion people and they can't control everything and watch everybody. Society has changed. Now there is the Internet, email, blogs, social networks, and the freedom of travel. Ideas, good and bad, spread quickly. As much as they try, it's difficult to maintain order with that many people.

There is also about a seventy percent divorce rate in China. Of the couples that are still married, many no longer live together. They believe finding good jobs is more important than staying together. The husband might get a job in one city and the wife find a good job in a city a thousand miles away. Then, when a national holiday comes, they each feel pressured to visit their respective parents, not each other. They also get hardly any time alone. They have one child and face a huge government fine of one year's salary if they have any more. Consequently, any subsequent children get aborted. The rich can afford to have more because they can afford to pay the fine. There is huge societal jealousy of the rich who can pay the fine and have another child. Recently, the rules were modified. The one-child policy was liberalized to permit a second child if either husband or wife was an only child. We hope this change will be a blessing to millions of Chinese families.

However, the one-child policy was designed to ease massive overcrowding in the country. That continues to be a serious problem. You have one hundred and forty to two hundred million workers from the countryside looking for work in the cities. Can you imagine the societal tension that creates? Many of the workers are not registered, so the actual numbers of peasants pouring into the urban areas may be much higher than reported. Then there are the problems between the rich and the poor, the educated and the uneducated.

Also, kids are being raised by grandparents while mom and dad go to work in the city. Many parents only see their child once a year. Many children grow up resenting their parents because they are not involved in their lives and daily problems. So you can see the need for values all across society. Many children live in school dormitories and only see their parents from Saturday evening to Sunday evening. There is so much academic pressure that instead of taking them to the park, parents enroll their one child in after-school and weekend tutoring classes.

Many children are raised going from one lecture to another their whole lives. Fortunately, things are beginning to change. There is a growing emphasis on more nurturing methods of education. We are so privileged to be involved in that transition. Our volunteer teachers and experts are welcomed and treated like heroes. Through friendships, mentoring, and spending time together our small team is having a very large impact.

We have the opportunity to be there and present the value of individual human life. We are instilling a belief in the dignity of the person. We're letting them know their worth, their treasures, and talents are not just academic. That's giving us the opportunity to help create an enormous paradigm shift in the largest nation in the world. We are amazed that through meeting the needs at a grassroots level, God has paved the way for His servants to have invitations to share in educational conferences for the nation. We are at a fulcrum point of changing education for millions of people.

Someone might ask why we need to be thinking about Asia. Why not just focus on needs in the United States? Forty percent of the world's population lives in just two countries, China and India. Both countries have been through strife, revolution, and enormous cultural pain; especially China. These include the Japanese invasion, the war between the Red and White armies, and the conversion to communism, followed by the Cultural Revolution. There are probably six hundred million people who live on two dollars a day or less. There are seven hundred million living in cities looking for a chance to succeed, and a chance to enjoy upward mobility. There are massive cultural, social, and economic needs.

We, as Christians, must understand it is not about us fundraising simply for this cause or that cause. God put the resources in some people's hands and their joy will come from moving those resources to where God has opened up an opportunity. God is always aligning people and opportunities so that people's needs may be met. The best kind of fundraising is matching up the need with those who have a passion to meet that need. Everyone gets the joy in that kind of situation. Regarding the fact that these people are in Asia, we have to remember Jesus teaches the kingdom of God isn't political. Earthly kingdoms come and go and political parties and nations rise and fall. We need to be concerned with meeting needs and helping people.

One final thing we have been able to do is help provide artificial limbs for people who need them. On one of our trips to China we met Yanni, a young Chinese medical doctor who, at age fourteen, lost a leg above the knee due to cancer. This young lady had been hobbling around on a rusty crutch in hospitals with wet floors; so there was a constant danger of her falling.

We saw her and decided we could get a leg made if we had the measurements. After getting the information that we needed, on our next trip I took her an artificial leg in my suitcase. It was my privilege to be the first one to help her take a step. Yanni was overjoyed! The first day she could walk on it. On the second day she walked to work. The third day she rode a bicycle to work. And the fourth day, she fell down because she got overly confident.

But she has, for the first time, learned to be social and come out of her shell. She has even learned to dance on her artificial leg and attend social events. She has also decided to educate herself about the Bible. Her desire is to serve people and share the message of faith, hope, and love.

In October of 2013, Yanni and her mom traveled from another part of China all the way to Beijing to see us. Her medical career is being blessed. We are in the process of getting her a new leg. She's worn the first one for eight years. She said, "No, get one for someone who has no leg." However, we compromised and ordered a replacement part for her old leg. We would still like to provide her a new leg one day.

Another person with whom we have worked is Kate. Kate's lower legs were crushed in the devastating Sichuan earthquake, May 12, 2008. She was in her apartment with her mother-in-law and ten-month-old baby. The apartment complex collapsed, trapping her under massive concrete slabs. Her baby died instantly. Her mother-in-law clung to life for ten more hours, but then passed away. It was pitch black. Kate's feet and ankles were mangled, slowly being crushed by the weight of the concrete slabs. Each aftershock increased the pressure. Kate decided things were so bad that it would be better if the rescuers did not find her and she died. About twenty-four hours after the collapse, she heard rescuers calling for her. She faced a life-and-death decision. Be silent and die; cry out and live. Kate chose life. She cried out. The rescuers uncovered most of her body but her feet were trapped. To save her life, they cut off both her legs about eight inches below the knees.

Kate's husband wasn't home at the time of the earthquake. When he got home, he waited outside the crumpled apartment to see if his wife, baby, and mother were alive or dead. When the rescuers got to Kate and reported she was alive, but crushed, and that his mother and the baby were dead, he abandoned Kate. Basically, he left her there to die.

In spite of the loss, Kate recovered in the hospital and was able to be fitted with simple artificial legs. Our team met her six months after the accident. She could not walk well, much less continue her career as a dance teacher. We arranged to provide her with state-of-the-art prosthesis. Two limb makers donated their time and money to provide Kate with new legs.

When she got her new legs, she was asked to speak about her experiences. Kate used all her earnings from those speaking events to rent an apartment for people who were injured in the earthquake. She has worked to find each one something to do so they could pay for their own prosthesis or the medical help they needed.

Jason Phillips in Lubbock and Tony Van Der Waarde in Vancouver worked tirelessly to restore Kate to a normal life. Tony has gone the second mile to provide Kate with a second and third set of legs for her performances on TV in China. Her follow-up care set up a contact with a limb company in China as well. That is a miracle story in itself, because she met her future husband, who works for the company.

Going back to when we first met Kate she noticed one of our team was wearing a cross on a necklace. She had searched for a

Bible since she was nine years old. Kate knew from movies there was some connection between crosses and the Bible. She summoned her courage and asked, "Do you know where I could get a Bible?"

Our team said, "Yes!" They gave her seven Bibles, enough for her and her friends. After eagerly reading her Bible, Kate put her faith in the loving God of the Bible. She has become a strong believer, growing from fear and shyness to dancing her way to national recognition as a heroic survivor of the devastating earthquake.

Recently, Kate remarried and I had the privilege of attending her wedding. Her tragedy has been redeemed and her life transformed. She has published a book about her experiences and her new life. It sells out everywhere across China. Millions have watched her on television and been encouraged by her story. The tragedy is behind her now and a new life lies ahead.

Yes, bad things happen. The world is a dangerous place. There is a devil and there is evil in the world. Bad things, terrible, horrible things happen all the time. If I could say that I've really learned one thing about life it is this: not all things are good, not all things are from God, but God is good. In fact, God is so good and so powerful and so full of love for His children that He can take our tragedies and disappointments and bring good out of them.

God is good. If you give your life and your future to God, and if you love Him, He will redeem the bad things that happen in your life. As it says in Romans 8:28-29, He will transform the terrible things that happen and use them for His glory. He may even go beyond that and make your recovery and transformation a platform for you to help others.

In the Old Testament book of Genesis, there is a story about Joseph and his eleven brothers. They were jealous of Joseph because their father liked him best. At first they wanted to kill him, but they finally settled on selling him to slave traders who took him to a distant country. Joseph was rejected and betrayed, but he never gave up. God stepped in and was able to use that terrible event to save and bless Joseph. With faith and trust in God's guidance and protection, Joseph became one of the most powerful men in Egypt, the most powerful nation at that time. His position allowed him to eventually save his family from a terrible famine. In Genesis 50, when Joseph revealed his identity to his brothers, he said, "What you meant for evil, God has used for good."

Chapter 22

A FINAL WORD: HOPE

Randy

Our culture tries to convince us this isn't true, but the fact is, everybody has problems. Problems are like weights in a gym. Pushing against them makes us stronger. We won't be able to successfully push against big problems that come into our lives until we learn to push against small ones. Problems are actually our friends because they make us stronger. Don't get angry when you are confronted with problems. Don't be resentful. Problems are an opportunity to learn, grow, and to strengthen our minds, our resolve, and develop a character trait called perseverance.

We live in a world where people both want and expect a perfect life, a life with no difficulties. We expect that if we press the right button or access the right app, all our concerns ought to go away. Life isn't like that. The reality is that we have problems every day. There is no perfect world, not in this life. That becomes crystal clear when even rich people, people who have all the things we think would make us happy, commit suicide because they are so miserable.

Life isn't perfect, so we have to decide here and now that the stresses of life will not defeat us. That's a very personal and important decision to make: *Problems will not defeat me. I will per-severe. I will overcome.* But where do you get the strength for that? People ask me all the time, "How do you keep hope alive when everything seems so hopeless? How do you survive the daily grind?"

In my own situation, the hope and vision of one day having a good life, along with support of friends, and spiritual faith, made it possible. Some people draw strength from their family or cultural history. People in China might say, "My grandparents went through the Cultural Revolution" or "My parents' survived prison." Others might say, "I had family members who nearly starved to death. They ate roots and trees and bushes to survive. If they can do that, I can survive what I'm going through." In the United States you might say, "My grandfather served in Korea or World War II. My dad fought in Vietnam. I come from a long line of problem solvers. I can do this."

Another source of strength is our hope for the future. Today will be over in less than twenty-four hours. Tomorrow is a new start. This problem is temporary. But I still have maybe seventy more years of life. I'm not going to let today's problem rob me of fifty or seventy years of living.

I encourage people to think of life as a discovery trip, an adventure, an exploration. We haven't found everything that life can hold. Don't miss tomorrow and all your tomorrows because of a problem today, no matter how big it seems. A problem is a chance to grow strong, to learn what doesn't work, and find what does. Become a life problem solver.

We can also draw encouragement from the stories of great overcomers in history. There are some fantastic stories in the last four- or five-thousand years of history that can help us be strong, help us overcome. The inventor Thomas Edison wanted to change electricity into visible light. He tried hundreds of experiments that didn't work, but he persevered. He kept on and today he is known as the father of electricity. He gave us the light bulb, the phonograph, and many other life-improving inventions. Millions of people from Africa to Beijing have enjoyed electric light because he refused to give up. That's how important perseverance is. Another overcomer was Jonas Salk. In his day, the world was tormented by polio. He set about to create a vaccine and discovered a way to prevent polio in hundreds of millions of people.

Looking back into ancient history, one of my favorite books is the Bible. It is full of people whose hope and faith helped them to overcome huge obstacles. With hope and faith and family, and a belief in Jesus Christ, I have seen so many problems overcome. Jesus Christ promises to be with me and never leave me. He holds me up and gives me courage and boldness. From the Christian perspective, we understand that God grants us outside power from Him because He loves us. We all need something to cling to, something to rely on that will help us see past the problems of now into the possibilities of tomorrow. When we face problems, we have to understand that they will pass, but the adventure will continue.

Sorrow and grief are some of the most powerful emotions any of us will ever have to work through, especially when we believe something we did is the root cause of the problem. To deal with that kind of emotion, we have to first realize the feelings are real; we have to admit our part in the problem, and not try to hide our guilt. We have to tell ourselves, "I caused a problem and I am responsible."

Taking responsibility can really help the healing process. Then decide to do whatever you can to make it right. Make an action plan so that you aren't drowning in sorrow, but rather swimming toward the shore. Each step of restitution, whether it's paying back a debt, or rebuilding a friendship, or taking a course over again at school, will bring healing.

There is a word in counseling, *catharsis,* which describes how healing it is to let out your secret sorrows and failures to a counselor or trusted friend. The very act of privately sharing your sorrow is a step toward healing. After someone has done those things, they can look for new ideas and new truth to change them so they never repeat the harmful action. For those who are Christians, they can draw strength from God to make that change.

There is a whole different kind of sorrow that is caused by others when they hurt us. I recommend people think about the loss and ask themselves, "Is it something I can change?" If you can change it, do it. If not, you have to declare the reality of the situation, allow yourself time to cry, and always keep in mind that your world will be different than it is now. The intensity of the pain will subside over time, no matter how permanent it seems at the moment. If we recognize our sorrow and grief, then we can also work to replace them with positive actions. That is the cure for many of our emotional problems.

We cannot defeat certain feelings, but we can replace those feelings with healthier feelings. We do that by replacing or changing our activities. For example, in this country we have tornadoes that have wiped out schools or buildings full of people. A parent might feel guilty they let their child go to school that day, even if there was no way they could have known what was about to happen.

In a school, they rush everyone to an interior room. I've heard that some people who have lost children in one of these terrible events are trying to change the laws. They want it to be required that every public building have Safe Rooms. They are focusing on making a positive difference as a way to honor their lost loved one. They can't bring back the children who were lost, but they can do something forceful, something positive, that will protect hundreds, maybe thousands, of other children in the future. We can't change the past, but we can change the future. Therefore, we must channel our energy from destructive survivor guilt to positive action.

In every adventure story you read, the heroes face great obstacles. It wouldn't be a great story if there weren't great obstacles to be overcome. What is the obstacle in your life today? How will you overcome that obstacle? We must decide not to sit around feeling bad and comparing our circumstances to someone else's. Your life is your adventure. Don't compare yourself to anyone else. In five years you probably won't even know where they are or what they're doing. It is your life!

See life as an adventure. You become stronger when you overcome problems. Our friends and family, as well as the world at large, benefit, too. You can choose to be a positive, encouraging people builder, business builder, and world improver. Isn't taking action better than sitting around feeling bad and accomplishing nothing?

Welcome problems. They make you strong. Solve problems. It makes you smart. Help others solve their problems. It makes you a leader. Learn from your problems. It makes you wise. As Mary Ann and I continue on the adventure of life, we don't know what the future holds. But we look forward to the adventure. We seek God's guidance. We look forward to the opportunities each new day will present. We want to see who God will put in our paths. We want to see what problems can be addressed in the lives of others through the resources the Lord has granted us.

Mary Ann

When Randy was injured, a lot of people asked if he was hurt in Vietnam. Again, there are people coming back from wars overseas who are amputees. My prayer is that this book will be an inspiration to them. Here is my husband Randy, who's lived for over forty years with artificial arms and had a great life. We want new amputees from the past ten years of war to know they can have a great life, too. Wholeness isn't about having all your body parts. It's how you see yourself and feel about yourself. Life is about what you *can* do, not what you *can't* do.

Randy

So what about Mary Ann and me? How does this affect how we live? Our lives have been dedicated to serving anyone who needs our help. We want to work with people who have a servant's heart. People are drawn to servant leaders. Humility is not a weakness. It is strength under control and the Biblical model of great leadership. We go to serve people. We pray for God's guidance before we do anything. If we believe that God wants us to get involved, we throw our lives into a situation with all of our energy. Today, we are at another beginning. It will be exciting to see where God leads us next. And we look forward to seeing you and hearing about what God is doing in your life.